PRAISE FOR *THE MAK...*

"Sheridan Voysey knows well the art of telling a story that takes you on a journey far away from where you are now. His latest book, a pilgrimage to rediscover himself, is just such a lyrical achievement. More importantly, though, his tale appeals to the journey of heart that all of us grapple with. Indeed, *The Making of Us* might just be the making of you."

—CLAIRE DIAZ-ORTIZ
Bestselling author and speaker

"It is a well-worn metaphor: life is a journey. While true, life is in fact far more like a pilgrimage. In *The Making of Us* Sheridan takes us on a beautiful and compelling trek to reveal how dissonance and disruption can call us into the delight of God. Brew a good mug of tea, wrap yourself in a warm blanket, and let this pilgrimage take you to the wonder that you, too, have been, are, and will always be on a great adventure to the Face of beauty."

—DAN B. ALLENDER, PHD
Professor of counseling psychology and founding president,
The Seattle School of Theology and Psychology

"So often as Christians we carefully and responsibly plan our way but forget that it is the Lord who directs our steps. Sheridan Voysey's reflection on the literal steps of his journey in search of the Lord's direction is a beautiful, evocative reminder that our lives as Christian saints are part of an eternal community, one not merely of our own place and time, and of a much larger story, one not merely of our own making."

—KAREN SWALLOW PRIOR
Author of *On Reading Well* and *Fierce Convictions*

"Traveling with his friend DJ and the invisible figure of Saint Cuthbert (a favorite of mine), Sheridan also journeys with the God he has been struggling to understand and hear clearly. Through typically honest and wonderful descriptions of his surroundings and inner musings, Sheridan warmly welcomes us to join this rich experience. An exceptional read."

—ADRIAN PLASS

Author of *The Shadow Doctor* and The Sacred Diary of Adrian Plass series

"Sheridan Voysey writes with depth and poetic imagery about the gifts that emerge when life doesn't go as planned. From his first question about where we fit into the world, to his last about how we desire to be remembered, he fills us with hope as he recounts his own search for purpose and calling, guided by the deep truth that we are always with God. This beautiful book will challenge you, guide you, call you to the countryside, and bring you back home to the truth that you, too, are always with God."

—BECCA STEVENS

Founder of Thistle Farms, author of *Love Heals*

"*The Making of Us* causes us to consider some of life's most searching questions: *Who am I? What should I do with my life? How can God know me completely, yet still love me utterly?* I found it a beautiful book, not just in its lyrical writing but in its gentle yet firm encouragement to press on with our journeys, even when we are doubting, fearful, and tired. This is a book to nourish our souls. I highly recommend it."

—ROB PARSONS, OBE

Founder and chairman, Care for the Family

"*The Making of Us* is a rich and nuanced exploration of vocation and identity. Who are we when we lose the status of a significant job, when we don't hit milestones alongside our peers, when our best laid plans don't come to pass? Does God have a unique purpose for each of us, and if so, how do we know what it is? Sheridan's hard-won wisdom is a gift to all of us who wrestle with these questions—to those at crossroads, to those who need help discerning the loving voice of

God. This beautifully crafted and lyrically written book is destined to become a cherished friend and companion to many."

—JO SWINNEY
Author of *Home*

"At one point in this stunning book Sheridan reflects, 'I want to craft words that captivate the heart and open eyes to see God.' In *The Making of Us* he does this with lyrical beauty. Through the pain, joy, heart-searching, and wrestling of these two blistered-feet pilgrims, the reader is drawn into an intimate and healing pilgrimage— attending, listening, questioning, and reflecting to finally discover the simple truth that what makes us valuable is that we are children of God."

—PAUL BUTLER
Bishop of Durham

"Sheridan proves to be an observant and wise travelling companion. This absorbing expedition along one of Britain's great pilgrim paths not only makes you feel like you're there but also encourages you to embark on your own inner exploration along the way. Well researched and beautifully crafted, this book itself is a journey worth making."

—CATHY MADAVAN
Speaker, writer, coach, and author of *Digging for Diamonds*

"As I read *The Making of Us*, I felt like Sheridan Voysey was reading my journal. He describes the losses and disappointments of adult life with aching clarity. Fortunately, through his remarkable pilgrimage, he also shows us how setbacks can be portals to a life of purpose— that 'Good things can come when you step into uncertainty.' He does it all with gorgeous prose that leaves you treasuring each sentence. Ride along on his journey. Like him, you won't come away unchanged."

—DREW DYCK
Author of *Your Future Self Will Thank You*

"This is a wonderful book—warm, life-giving, encouraging, while discussing big issues and asking big questions. Sheridan speaks with integrity and authenticity as he helps us consider our response when life begins to look different from what we hoped for or planned. I finished *The Making of Us* with a renewed sense of God's great love for me, his daughter, and reminded that he can use even the most painful of experiences to shape us into the people he created us to be."

—KATE WHARTON
Assistant national leader, New Wine network;
vicar of St. Bart's Roby; and author of *Single Minded*

"Having faced a broken dream with courage, Sheridan Voysey sets off on a pilgrimage to rediscover his calling. What he finds—amid blisters, aching muscles, and broken nights' sleep—is a deeper truth altogether. Whether or not you can strap on your walking boots, you'll find Sheridan a warm and winsome companion with whom to delve into matters of identity, calling, and hearing God's voice. One to savor, ponder, and share with others. I loved it!"

—AMY BOUCHER PYE
Author of *Finding Myself in Britain*

"Sheridan Voysey is an exquisite, masterful writer, transporting us to the northeast coast of England to join him on his long trek. The deep, relatable reflections in these pages stopped me in my hectic, hurried days and gave me space to drink in truths about issues of substance, and untangle wrong thinking about living as a follower of Jesus. Rarely do any of us live out our 'Plan A' lives, and in *The Making of Us* I found perspective, hope, and wisdom through a wonderfully written blend of history, theology, and life lessons."

—VIVIAN MABUNI
Speaker and author of *Warrior in Pink* and *Open Hands, Willing Heart*

THE
MAKING
OF US

ALSO BY SHERIDAN VOYSEY

Resurrection Year
Resilient
Unseen Footprints
Open House (3 volumes)

THE
MAKING
OF US

WHO WE CAN BECOME WHEN LIFE
DOESN'T GO AS PLANNED

SHERIDAN VOYSEY

W PUBLISHING GROUP

AN IMPRINT OF THOMAS NELSON

Published in Nashville, Tennessee, by W Publishing, an imprint of Thomas Nelson.

Thomas Nelson titles may be purchased in bulk for educational, business, fund-raising, or sales promotional use. For information, please e-mail SpecialMarkets@ ThomasNelson.com.

ISBN 978-0-7180-9423-2 (TP)
ISBN 978-0-7180-9559-8 (eBook)

Library of Congress Cataloging-in-Publication Data

Library of Congress Control Number: 2018961500

Printed in the United States of America
19 20 21 22 23 LSC 10 9 8 7 6 5 4 3 2 1

For
Clare, Melanie,
Curtis and Amy, Graham and Rachel,
James and Beth

CONTENTS

AUTHOR'S NOTE

We open our eyes for the very first time. We wiggle our hands and kick our feet. We shake the rattle, stack the blocks, pick up the crayon and color the walls. We crawl and climb and prod and peek, and begin to discover what we're capable of.

Soon we're whizzing paper planes around the room and pretending to be pilots, or drawing wheels on boxes and pretending to be drivers, or nursing sick dolls and pretending to be mothers, exploring the possibilities of who we could be.

Next come books, classes, exams, and crushes, followed by majors to pick and career paths to choose. And as we set out in life and get our first job, or walk down the aisle and have our first child, or chase some dreams and taste some success, we may begin to discover what we're here for. We may begin to find our purpose.

I used to think this search for a calling in life ended here. As we prayed hard, pursued our passions, and followed what we did well, we would find the one big thing we were meant to do with our lives and then spend the rest of our days doing it. Now I'm not so sure. Few people in their forties end up doing what they planned in their twenties.

Because life is precarious and things change. Perhaps the company folds, or the marriage ends, or the kids leave home, or the accident happens, or the role no longer fits, or success no longer matters. Any idea we had about our place in the world vanishes like mist, and we find ourselves asking *What am I here for?* all over again.

Such times can leave us disillusioned and confused. But they can also lead to the finest treasures. Because when life as we know it ends, new adventures can begin. When identity is lost, we can discover who we really are. The adversity we despise can release our greatest gifts into the world. And all the details of our lives—from the first wiggle of our hands to the difficult events that brought us to this point—can prove to be more significant than we've realized.

Beautiful things can emerge from life not going as planned. It can even be the making of us.

Sheridan Voysey

CHAPTER 1

A SOUL ADRIFT

The traffic lights flashed yellow, and I slowed to a stop. That's when it caught my eye: a white plastic grocery bag floating in the air, stuck in the middle of the freeway. Rising and falling, it blew this way and that, trapped in the *whoosh* of the traffic. It danced and swirled and curled and did somersaults, ballooning like a parachute, then collapsing flat. That bag flittered like a spirit, like a shirt without a body, drifting and directionless, prey to each gust of wind.

This spectacle continued for some time until a sports car raced past. And with a sudden flourish, the white plastic bag was ripped from the air. It rushed to the car's side, swept up into its slipstream, and began following it down the freeway. And there it stayed, fluttering behind the bumper, in the grip of an unknown driver, getting carried somewhere far away.

SEPTEMBER 2013

Sprawling countryside rushes past my window—fields of tan and paddocks of green, sheep-peppered hills and hay bales dotting tractor trails, old barns, stone walls, wooden gates, and streams. It's gray outside, but the scenery still inspires.

"Welcome to the 1:15 p.m. service to Edinburgh," the conductor says over the speakers. "Our next station is Newcastle upon Tyne."

The girl sitting next to me has her earbuds in. The guy across the table stares into his laptop. A grandmotherly soul sits across the aisle to my right. She gives a little smile to each passenger as they board, makes friendly muttering noises as they find their seats, then returns to her crossword puzzle once they've settled in. Bless her.

My wife, Merryn, and I have been in England two years now, long enough to have seen its faults yet still love the place. For this is a land of rolling hills and winding rivers, of castles, cathedrals, and cozy towns. There's history in every brick, a story on every corner, as a visit to our home city of Oxford shows. Handel premiered his oratorios in Oxford's Sheldonian Theatre, and Shakespeare used to lodge at the nearby Crown Tavern. William Penn studied in Oxford before founding Pennsylvania, and John Wesley once preached in its churches. John Donne, Oscar Wilde, and Dorothy Sayers lived here for a time, and C. S. Lewis wrote his books in a house up the road. I never tire of wandering Oxford's old streets, wondering in whose footsteps I'm walking.

But two years is enough to miss what you've left behind.

And I don't just mean the family and friends we've left in Australia, or the blue skies and sunshine, or Sydney's glistening harbor that's always so full of life. I mean the sense of knowing your place in the world. The sense of knowing where you fit.

The grandmotherly soul looks up from her crossword as an eccentric couple walks through the carriage. The man is probably in his eighties, the woman a little younger. He wears a yellow shirt with mauve stripes, hiking sandals with tennis socks, and white suspenders holding up corduroy trousers that are too short in the leg but too wide in the hip. His wild gray hair points in all directions and is trying to escape out his nose and ears. Her sand-colored hair is pulled back in a bun. She wears blue trousers, supermarket sneakers, and a sweater as pink as the rose of her cheeks. They slide into seats opposite the grandmother, who approves with much muttering.

The rose-cheeked woman pulls from her bag two small fruit juices, the kind with the little twisty straws stuck on the side. A plastic-wrapped stack of jam sandwiches comes out next, which the man eyes with interest.

"How many of these are mine then?" he asks, a little too loudly.

"Three halves," she says. "But wait . . ."

The woman rummages in her bag and finds some napkins. They're printed with bright blue cupcakes with red icing—the kind you get at children's parties. She places one in each lap, he scrunches a third into his collar, and they begin to munch and sip and drop their crumbs. I almost expect party hats to come out next. Maybe you reach an age where the fear of looking ridiculous dissipates.

I have my journal out, attempting to scribble down what's

going on within me. The rocking of the train makes it hard to write, and, if I'm honest, the words I scrawl aren't just messy but blurred. I must face the truth: I need glasses. Gray flecks have appeared in my dark-blond hair, too, and after years of being skinny, my waist has expanded. It's becoming obvious to all that I've passed the age of forty.

Friends farther along the path tell me the forties can be a time of reckoning. With mortgages to pay, children to feed, expectations to meet, and aging parents to care for, one can feel constrained by responsibility. The dreams of our twenties may not have come to pass; the failures of our youth may be catching up with us. And with time rolling on and choices hard to change, disillusionment can set in.

But my friends also tell me the forties can be rich—a time to lead and flourish and make one's mark. We've honed our skills and have expertise to offer. We've faced a few battles and have wisdom to share. Our bodies can still keep pace with what our minds can imagine. It's also the age, they say, when we begin to stop worrying about what others think of us.

I'll find out soon enough how right my friends are, but I'm pretty sure I'm not in some midlife crisis yet. The restless feelings I scrawl in that journal haven't come as some slow-rising tide of middle-age disappointment. They've come quickly, like a crashing wave—the result of one life-defining event.

"Arriving at Newcastle upon Tyne," the announcer says as we begin to slow.

In total, today's trip will be over seven hours long. I'd gotten a bit lost in London this morning, looking for the right Underground line to reach this train, zigzagging the passageways beneath Paddington Station with another guy to find the platform.

"What do you do?" I'd asked him as we walked together.

"I'm a software engineer," he said. "And you?"

"Well, I guess I'm a writer," I said, looking for words. "But I used to be in radio."

Why do you do that? I wonder now. *Why do you always tell people what you* used *to be?*

Because I don't know who I am now, I realize.

For years I'd had my life figured out, with a settled career and a clear sense of purpose. Now I have neither, and I feel directionless—like a plastic bag I once saw floating along the freeway. It rose and fell, blew this way and that, tossed about by the *whoosh* of each passing car.

—————

It doesn't take long to wind through Newcastle's bridges and buildings, slip past its terrace-house suburbs, and get back into farmland. From here we cross hills, valleys, meadows, and pastures. If you were to look down from the sky, you'd see how they all join up like a patchwork quilt—each field a patch sewn together by hedgerows.

"The next station is Berwick-upon-Tweed," comes the announcement.

I've ridden this train just once before—a dozen years ago during a holiday to the UK when we'd visited a friend in Edinburgh. Merryn and I had talked about our dreams on this train—about writing books and having kids and starting national radio shows. So much has happened since. One of those dreams has been fulfilled, one has been broken, and a third has come and gone.

—————

I've been on the radio a lot recently, but as the guest, not the host—doing publicity for a book I wrote that came out a few months ago. A phone interview last week on an American show comes to mind and makes me smile.

"I have to tell ya somethin'," the host had said in her deep Southern accent as we waited to go live. "You have given me one of the best quotes of my week from your book. Ya know which one it is?"

"Is it the one that goes, 'A greater tragedy than a broken dream is a life forever defined by it'? People seem to like that one."

"No, not that one," she said. "It's where you say, 'You're never as old as you once were, and never as young as you think you're gonna be.' Do you remember sayin' that?"

I was silent for a few seconds. Not only had I not said it, I didn't even know what it meant. My host must've been quoting another author, which wasn't a great start for our interview. I tried to let her down easy.

"Perhaps you're paraphrasing me and I can't recognize it . . ."

"Yeah, perhaps I'm paraphrasing you."

The show had begun and my host had been funny, friendly, and proven soon enough that she'd read the right book. "You and your wife tried all those years to have a baby," she said, recounting the story. "And you tried everything, I mean *everything*, to start your family—in-vitro fertilization, adoption, special diets, prayer. You pursued that dream for so long . . ."

"Ten years," I said.

"And toward the end it looked like you had what you'd prayed for," she added. "I have to tell ya, Sheridan—when I read the bit about the phone call on Christmas Eve, and them tellin' your wife she wasn't pregnant after all, and her puttin' the phone down and curlin' up on the bed in tears . . . well, that had *me* in tears."

"You're not alone," I said. "Few people get through that chapter with dry eyes."

"And here's what I don't get," she added. "You and your lovely wife tried all those years to have a baby and couldn't. And me—well, I just spit them babies out!"

I nearly choked on my glass of water.

"I mean, Vince only has to look at me a certain way and the next thing I know, I'm bein' wheeled into the delivery ward. Ya know what I'm sayin'?"

"I get it," I said, laughing now. "It's an unfair world."

"But then came your Resurrection Year. Tell the listeners about that."

"After that call on Christmas Eve, we decided to start our lives again," I said. "Merryn really only had two dreams in life: to become a mother and to live overseas. When the first dream died, it was time for her to have the consolation prize. And when she was offered her ideal job at Oxford University, we took it as a sign to leave Australia and come to England."

"But that came at a cost to you, didn't it?"

"Well, I had this radio show by then—"

"A national show, which was *your* dream job. And you gave it up for your wife . . ."

A point like this came in most interviews, and I had to navigate it carefully so as not to appear the hero. Yes, that radio show had been my dream job—a God-given dream that had taken a decade to materialize. Yes, that show had been special—exploring Christian faith with secular people in creative ways. Yes, it had broken my heart to leave it—that show was my baby.

"But don't think I gave it up with saintly joy and unwavering faith," I told the host. "I wrestled and doubted and sulked about it. And it wasn't like Merryn hadn't made sacrifices for me. Besides, when you've held your wife every night as she's sobbed over what she can't have, and an opportunity comes up for something she can—well, only the most callous person would stop her from having it."

"But it shook up your writing career, too, right?"

"British publishers turned my books down because I wasn't known here like I was in Australia. This book ended up with a US publisher. Thank God for you Americans."

"You can get a pizza to your door here faster than an ambulance," the host chuckled, "but at least we give folks a chance. Hey, we're runnin' outta time, but I gotta ask you this: how is your wife doin' now?"

"Those ten years were like wandering in the wilderness," I said, "but for Merryn, coming to Oxford has been like entering the promised land. A job is no replacement for a child, of course, but it's been the new beginning she needed."

"And you? Are things looking up with this new book an' all?"

I had a book contract with a major publisher, something every writer wants. But strangely, this had only added to my confusion. I'd spent years giving people reasons to believe in God, and now I was writing about broken dreams and unanswered prayers. It was very different territory. Was this the new direction my life was to take, or just a momentary diversion? If only I could look down from above and see how my past and present fit together.

"I'm definitely on a new path," I said, "and I'm not sure

where it's leading. But unexpected journeys can take you to good places."

———

The sky is more dramatic now. Full of contrast, full of might. The ashen blanket that covered us all day has rippled into waves, then parted into pillows of deep gray cloud rimmed in white. Fingers of light break on the horizon, and I can see the ocean now. Drops of rain hit the window and make little trails across the glass.

It's time, I think. *I'm ready for this.* Abram embarked on his sacred trek and found his place in history. The Israelites walked their wilderness path and reached their promised land. The wise men took to their sandy trail and found where to lay their gifts. Cleopas's eyes were opened wide as he walked the Emmaus road. Scripture is full of sacred journeys—from heavens to earth, from graves to skies—and as countless saints have proven since, a walk with God can bring clarity.

Yes, it's time. I'm ready to go on pilgrimage.

My backpack sits in the luggage rack by the door. It's as light as I could make it and holds only the essentials: T-shirts, underwear, water bottle, raincoat, Band-Aids, painkillers, toothbrush, Bible. I've brought my camera, too (an essential in my book), and a small packet of cheap dark chocolate.

Like those pilgrims of old, I won't journey alone. My good friend DJ will join me for the trek, and another, historical, figure will be "present" as we walk. Revered as a saint, a miracle worker, and a holy man, the famed medieval monk Cuthbert is as integral to this land as its wind and its waves. Consulted by kings

———

but a friend to paupers, a hermit at heart but a missionary by calling, a healer of bodies and a revealer of mysteries, Cuthbert traipsed this land with the Gospels in his hand, praying through his tears and preaching up a storm, baptizing thousands, and changing the face of Britain. Through Cuthbert and other saints like Aidan, Hilda, and Bede, Christianity took root in the north English heart and changed the course of history.

This is new terrain for me—spiritually, I mean. I have never attempted a pilgrimage before, the concept being quite foreign to the average Australian. And I've never had much interest in saints, let alone Cuthbert. But the more I've looked into pilgrimage, the more I've felt drawn to do one, and the more I've learned about Cuthbert, the more I've wanted to know. And there's a good reason to explore his world now.

"Look out there," the wooly-haired man says, jam on his fingers, pointing toward the sea. "Past the castle on the hill. See it? That's Lindisfarne."

And there it is, barely a smudge on the window from this distance—the cradle of indigenous English Christianity and the starting point of my journey, Holy Island Lindisfarne. Founded in the seventh century as a place of spirituality and mission, the gospel flames tended here by Cuthbert and others spread across the land and to the four corners of the world.

"That's where I'm going," I say, breaking the great unwritten rule of keeping to oneself on British public transport.

"To Holy Island?" says the eccentric gent.

"Ooh, it's lovely there," says the grandmother.

"What takes you there, then?" says the guy with the laptop.

And I wonder why I haven't spoken up sooner.

I manage to explain the basics of my trip before the train

slows down and I must gather my things, hoist on my pack, and leave. I'm sent on my way with nods and farewells and the wave of a half-eaten jam sandwich, while my once-silent travel companions share their childhood visits to the island with each other.

———

"I thought about emigrating to Australia once," the taxi driver tells me.

"Really?" I say, enjoying his Scots-tinged accent.

"Aye. I even rang the Australian Embassy for details. They asked me if I had a criminal record. I said, 'Why? Is it still an entry requirement?'"

I've heard the convict joke before, but it's still funny coming from him. Rob tells me he was born in Berwick and has been a taxi driver for years. His punch lines come subtly, with just a smile and a wink. There'll be a few of them as he drives me to Beal, the little mainland village near the crossing to Lindisfarne.

"So you're walking from Holy Island to Durham," Rob says, his r's softly rolled. "That's not a wee trek."

"About 115 miles," I say.

"And how long have ye got to do it in?"

There's some time pressure on our trip. After Cuthbert's death in 687, the Lindisfarne monks crafted one of the era's most precious works of art in his honor—the Lindisfarne Gospels. Now thirteen hundred years old, this exquisitely illustrated book, so luminous in detail but fragile in page, is on display at Durham University. It's a rare event—the frail Gospels barely leave their vacuum-sealed box in the British Library. And the display is ending soon.

———

"We'll have eight days to get to Durham before the Gospels go back to London," I tell Rob.

"Better you than me," he says. "But you'll have a good stay on Lindisfarne anyhow—visitin' the castle and the ruins and all them nightclubs." Wink.

Lindisfarne has just 160 residents and a small number of guest rooms. The single road to it floods at high tide, limiting access to a few hours each day. Naturalists visit for its flora and fauna. Families visit for a pleasant day out. Pilgrims come for its solitude and quiet. If throbbing beats and lasers are your thing, you've taken a wrong turn.

The tide is high for the rest of the day, so I must spend the night in Beal. Rob pulls up to the inn I've booked, which looks like a small English pub.

"Is this a reputable place?" I ask, seeing there's little else around.

"Ooh, aye," he says, looking serious now. "You'll have no problems here. Not since they bolted the tables to the floor."

And he smiles.

My room is neat, tidy, three-star quality—white sheets, lemon walls, pine table, kettle—with a window view of the parking lot. It's not the most mystical of beginnings, but the delay onto the island has its benefits. Had the tide been low, I'd have let Rob drive me over tonight, missing the mudflats walk I'll make in the morning.

I put down my pack and sit on the bed. It's been a long day. A long year. DJ won't be here for another two days, so the time is right for some pre-trek solitude. *And I can start now*, I think. Right in this room, with its plain walls and pedestrian views.

I take off my boots and kneel down. The posture might help me focus.

Oh God, I ask for . . .

It's quiet in the room, but not within. Deep inside I'm an Indian street at peak hour, all yelling and jostling and noise. I hear echoes of conversations with folks on trains, with software engineers and southern radio hosts. I feel the empty space of a dream now gone and a soul longing for its replacement. And I replay those conversations and say different things, and I feel that soul torn in so many directions. I return as my prayers elbow their way through this mass of memories and questions.

. . . the book . . .

So much now rides on the book selling well. Or at least that's how it feels. My deepest desire is to see readers' lives changed, but publishers look for sales success, too, and if the numbers aren't there, future books are in jeopardy. My first royalty report came in the mail the other day. It didn't carry the greatest of news.

. . . and the future . . .

Some may find the free-floating life fun—to rise and fall and dance and swirl and be carried on the currents of whatever fate brings. But I've always wanted my life to build toward *one big thing*, not flit between many possibilities. I don't want to be prey to outside forces, pushed by the *whoosh* of every idea or whim. I want a new plan to follow, clear focus—new direction. Somewhere down the road that white plastic bag lies in a gutter, all trampled and trodden.

Give me a new dream, God; a new purpose, a new calling . . .

Once full of dreams, my imagination is now blank. Once

full of ambition, I'm now empty. And my deepest fear is that this won't change—that for the rest of my days I'll drift without aim, achieve little of significance, and leave without a trace.

These are such self-absorbed prayers. I seek your will alone. Maybe if I just . . .

Just be present, Sheridan.

A sense.

A thought.

A voice.

A whisper.

Words full of weight but lighter than air.

No, it was softer than a thought, and deeper than a feeling. A voice heard with the heart, not an ear.

Just be present before me. This is your first task in life.

I release a deep breath and my shoulders unwind. I sink into the mattress. Holy gravity. The remedy has come. The answer—my God.

And all the memories and questions and echoed conversations, and all the tensions and requests and worries, are hushed in an instant to inner quietness. Wordless, requestless presence.

Moses stood in his Tent of Meeting. Elijah waited on his mountaintop. Anna prayed in the temple each day. Mary sat at the feet of her Lord.[1] Each came seeking, but first listened and was present. And each one received what he or she came for.

The pilgrimage hasn't begun, but I've had my first epiphany.

Seek a new dream if you wish. Ask for a new purpose or calling. But one task precedes them that will last into eternity:

Your first calling in life is to be with God.

CHAPTER 2

SAND AND STARS

The air is surprisingly still, comfortably cool, mildly salty, quiet. Given the leaden clouds that cascade above, row upon row of them marching to the horizon, I expect a rumble of thunder any moment. But a wisp of breeze is all I hear, and the rustle of my pack, and the sound of my breath.

I stretch out a bare foot to take a step. It's embarrassingly white from lack of exposure to the elements. Such a city boy.

The water is cool on the toes. I venture out a few meters. A centimeter of receding tide still covers the sand and has turned the mudflats into a mirror that stretches for miles. I am standing on water. I am walking on sky. I slosh forward, making ripples in upturned clouds.

Lead me, God.

Lead me.

A row of wooden poles marks the Pilgrim's Way ahead, the most ancient path to Lindisfarne. Hundreds of those poles stand tall and straight, seemingly suspended in air.

Holy Island is like a lamb cutlet in shape, with a bone of sand dunes leading to a body of pastures, homes, and ancient ruins. This path, a little over three miles long, is the direct route to the island's center.

The sand is firm. I follow the poles. Patches of blue break through the silvery cloud I walk on, and sandbars begin to emerge like tiny islands. There's a refuge ahead for those who misjudge the tides—a cubby house of sorts, on stilts with a ladder. Two people, my only companions on the path, stand looking at it.

Speak, Lord.

Speak.

Islands can represent danger in popular imagination. In *Robinson Crusoe* an island becomes a prison for a shipwrecked sailor, in *Lord of the Flies* it's where children become beasts, and reality TV shows portray them as untamed jungles to be survived. Or we see islands as symbols of adventure. *Treasure Island* is a place of bounty, Thomas More's island *Utopia* is the ideal society, and glossy brochures sell us island getaways full of bikinis, daiquiris, and fun.

But in northern England, islands are more rugged rock than palm frond, and while history-making peril would surely visit Lindisfarne, isles like this meant something else to Cuthbert and his friends. Connected by earth but separated by sea, removed from the world but just an arm's stretch away, islands could be havens of heaven in a brutal age—places not of danger or adventure but of retreat.

"A beautiful morning for it," the man by the refuge says as I approach.

"You do miss the crowds on a weekday," the woman next to him says.

They are both in their fifties and dressed for walking, with raincoats on and trousers rolled up. But while my boots dangle from my pack by their laces, the couple has kept theirs on. I want to rush over, rip those shoes off, and force their pasty white soles to feel the squelch of the mud and grit of the sand. Clearly I'm a convert.

"Oxford, you say," the man remarks after we exchange pleasantries and mention where we've traveled from.

"We have a son at university there," the woman says as we walk on together, "and another just graduated from Cambridge."

"Impressive," I note. Getting both children into Britain's top universities is a feat. "What are their subjects?"

"David is doing classics," the man says, "and hopes to teach when he's done. He's always known he wanted to be a university lecturer."

"And that's what he'll become," adds the woman.

My pack weighs heavy on my shoulders, not comfortably on my hips as it should. I reposition the bag, tighten the waist straps, and think of all the Me's I've wanted to be over the years—the graphic artist of my childhood, the nightclub DJ of my teens, the syndicated radio host of my twenties, the Christian leader of my thirties with my books, columns, and international reach.

At times I'd envisioned a social-worker Me who could foster troubled children, or an entrepreneurial Me who could build a mighty organization. There was Me the pastor, Me the evangelist, Me the prophet and wonder worker. A few of these Me's appeared for a time. Many were borrowed from biographies—tried on for size but found to fit as awkwardly as this pack.

"And your other son," I asked, "who graduated?"

"James read history," the man says, "but isn't sure what he wants to do yet."

"He's a bit directionless," says the woman.

"Hasn't worked out who he is," says the man.

I step around some stones lodged in the sand.

"That can take some time," I say.

———

I follow the floating poles. The cascading gray drifts away, leaving a glassy vista of white and blue. The water mirrors the sky like a Rorschach test turned sideways—as if the colors of heaven had been folded over the horizon and pressed into earth.

My left foot slips on a slick of mud. I lunge sideways as my boots swing around and throw me off balance. I'm traveling light—one has to on the Pilgrim's Way—but my pack has added weight that pulls me down. I stumble and slide and flail my arms but manage to avoid a fall. The couple doesn't notice. They're way back, inspecting something, their toothy boots keeping them vertical. What thrills they're missing.

All marks of my scuffle soon vanish, smoothed flat by the water's hand. What history is hidden by these twice-daily tides? Centuries of footprints striding to this island. Bundles of burdens carried across these flats. Two hundred years after his death, monks walked this path with Cuthbert's coffin on their shoulders, rescuing their saint and the Lindisfarne Gospels from the Vikings. That image seems true of pilgrimage in general: while every pilgrim must travel light, few travel without a burden.

It may not be a best seller yet, but that book I wrote has drawn an unexpected response. Through e-mails and letters readers have shared their heartbreaks and secrets—words that linger in my mind as I walk:

> We were given the gift of pregnancy three times and on each occasion heard the life-shattering words: "I'm sorry, but your baby has no heartbeat . . ."

> One December morning my husband went to work. By that afternoon he'd been arrested on charges of child sexual abuse . . .

> We came here to serve God, and it nearly cost us our lives . . .

> My husband had so many affairs I gave up caring . . .

Among the trials in those letters have come bright bursts of hope:

> Tonight I surrendered my dreams of marriage and a family, and have found a new peace about being single . . .

> My son has Asperger's, and my marriage is in tatters. But I've just read your book and feel I can start again now, and find God again too . . .

———

A light has switched on. I'm going to grab life with both hands. I won't be defined by my broken dreams anymore . . .

And some messages have simply brought a smile:

I don't often cry when I read, but your book has broken me. The problem is, I work in a pub, and being a crying bartender isn't good for my street cred.

But it's another batch of letters that echo loudest this quiet morning:

If I can't become a mother, life seems pointless . . .

Every idea I had about who I could become has been stripped away . . .

My life feels like a jigsaw puzzle that's been thrown into the air . . .

I no longer know who I am or why I'm here . . .

I sidestep some stones, cross a marshy patch, set my feet on dry sand, and look back. It's taken an hour and a half to reach Lindisfarne's shore. I sit down for a rest, wipe the mud from my legs, and drink in those reflections once more.

Few travel without a burden.

Since every dream carries with it an identity, a broken dream can shatter one's sense of self. Those letters have revealed a crisis shared by many. Each of us searches for a new Me when life doesn't go as planned.

———

I find a twig in the grass and scribble shapes in the sand. And after another deep breath and gaze at the view, I lace up my boots, gather up my pack, and carry those heartbreaks and secrets over the dune.

———

I find the Manor House Hotel and check into my room—a simple single-bed affair with a sash window looking out to Lindisfarne's harbor. The soft light outside turns the window scene into a pastel sketch. Like Lucy and Edmund, I'm beckoned through the frame into its world. I take my camera and rush out.

I explore the harbor first, with its small working jetty, its moored trawlers and stacked lobster pots, admiring its old wooden dinghies with their flaky blue paint, and its sheds made of upturned boats cut in half like bread loaves.

I next walk out to the sixteenth-century castle that rises sheer like a volcano, clutch its worn wooden rail, and climb the rough stone steps to the top for its view. I roam the surrounding fields, their spongy grass kept short by dozens of grazing sheep, then circle back to survey the old shops in the village's quiet main street.

Hours pass, my lens sucking in those pastels. I wander around the ruins of the twelfth-century priory built on the site of the first monastery, its ancient red-brick arches pocked and gritty from age. From there I visit St. Mary's, the island's parish church, with its large wooden sculpture of Cuthbert's monks carrying his coffin across the mud.

By late afternoon I'm tiptoeing across the rocks at low tide to the tiny isle of Hobthrush. Better known as Cuthbert's

Island, this was where Cuthbert came for solitude when the monastery's activity became too much.

I sit down on a rocky ledge and dangle my feet over the lapping water, the breeze light and scented with seaweed. Soon something swirls down on my left. A soft, small snout breaks the water's surface, followed by long white whiskers and eyes like onyx. It's a gray seal, all puppylike and inquisitive. It sniffs the air to catch my scent and looks me up and down.

The day has been good. My survey of the island has been valuable, and the photography fun. But as the sunlight fades, I feel the space of something missed.

I had begun the day as a pilgrim but ended it a tourist, trading my prayers for camera clicks. I had rushed about on the island of retreat, seeing many good things but perceiving few deeply. There's a time to be a tourist, but this time is for prayer. I had trekked those flats asking God to speak, then left little room to listen.

Tomorrow will be different.

The water is rising. I should get back soon. But with the sun hanging low and my whiskered friend sloshing about, I don't want to move.

A second seal swims up, swishing its fins and blowing wet air from its nostrils. Thousands of its kin gather on an outlying sandbank and start to sing—a midpitch wail, echoey and distant, a song heard in these regions every evening.

A bell sounds from St. Mary's to gather us for evensong. I decide to go and determine to walk there slowly, attentively, without rush or hurry.

I push myself up from the ledge, brush the dirt off my trousers, start ambling down the slope—and begin to run.

I'd heard the tide could rise quickly, but this is ridiculous. I hop over the last unsubmerged rocks, then plunge shin-deep into the sea, splashing my way to shore, soaking my boots and jeans.

I arrive late to St. Mary's, the wet soles of my squelching shoes squeaking on the floor as loudly as those crooning seals.

Slowly. Attentively. Without rush or hurry. One foot placed gently after the other, leaving a single line of prints on the shore. Waves slide over the sand like soft blue bedsheets and leave frothy white bubbles as they recede. The northern wind is cold and gusty and makes the grass on the sand dunes dance.

Teach me, God.

Teach me.

A new day. I started it this morning watching dark clouds flee from an expanding horizon of blazing orange, and after early prayers at St. Mary's, I'd returned for breakfast as beams of light hit the ocean. Now I walk on Holy Island's north shore, a band of beach along the bone of the cutlet. The sea on my left is ultramarine blue, and tan and charcoal sands sweep ahead like brushstrokes.

I feel the bubbles pop beneath my feet and think about church this morning. I'd fared better than yesterday, when my late arrival meant missing the vicar's instructions on how the service cards worked. I'd recited the wrong prayers, continued when others paused, missed my turn to read aloud, sat when others stood. As a teenage convert to evangelical faith with its extemporaneous prayer and passion, I'd been a liturgical embarrassment in wet shoes. But this morning I'd participated with greater dignity.

We'd read verses from Proverbs 8, where wisdom cries out to be noticed. "I was born before the oceans were created," she says, before mountains were formed and the first hand-fuls of soil scattered.[1] And as an artist's soul can be revealed through her paintings, so this divine wisdom can be glimpsed in creation:

"I was there when he established the heavens . . ."

"I was there when he set the clouds above . . ."

"I was there when he set the limits of the seas . . ."

Attend, Sheridan.

I stop still and face the ocean.

Attend to what you see.

The salty north wind hits my face, powerful yet benign. It tousles my hair and chills my wet feet. It sends sand grains scuttling across the ground, stirs those waters to crest, crash, and hiss, and blows large clouds effortlessly across the sky. I gulp that ocean breeze deep into my lungs, then sit down in the squelchy sand.

I am alone on the beach. There isn't another soul for miles. There are no boats, boardwalks, jetties, or hotels—just raw sea, sky, and shore.

Open my eyes, God. Show me more.

I gaze at those waves, so dark and choppy. Another world lies beneath them: schools of salmon and mackerel surging to and fro; shimmering pilchard, cod, redfish, and herring. In those waters are delicacies like lobsters and mussels. At its depths are starfish, kelp forests, and corals. Farther out you'll find dolphins, stingrays, and minke whales, and waves so large they can drive tankers to the sea floor.

And the sky I cast my eyes to—a myriad of wonders lies beyond it: millions of suns and trillions of planets in our Milky Way, a galaxy that is one of one hundred billion others, all twirling around like carousels. Right now the moon spins around us at 2,300 miles an hour, while we spin around the sun at 67,000 miles an hour, while our sun spins around our galaxy at 483,000 miles an hour, while our galaxy races through the universe at a million clicks and more. There's more going on than those clouds above show.

I take a scoop of sand and let it slip through my fingers. Each grain is a wonder in itself. For if we were to leap from the edge of the cosmos and fly around the planets, slip through Saturn's rings, pass Jupiter and Mars, dodge the moon, pierce the sky, rush toward this shore, and dive into one of these grains, we would see another world again. We would glide past buzzing atoms, sail through electron storms, crack open protons, and find our universe in miniature form, with quarks dashing around in nanoscopic space like shooting stars.

This world is beautifully arranged, finely designed, intricately tuned, wisely made. And to think: if Earth were a little closer to the sun or if gravity were dialed down a few notches, the whole wonderful thing would dissolve in a second.[2]

"I stared at my screen this morning," Merryn had said a few years ago, our journey for a family not yet over. Her eyes were red. "And I wondered if this is it."

"If this is what?" I'd asked, watching her chin quiver.

"If this is all my life will be since we're not going to have kids—just spreadsheets and numbers and analysis of data. Dry. Boring. Meaningless."

And with an unusual boldness, I'd said that was a lie. Merryn's life would never be meaningless, pointless, or futile.

Because while I have many questions over its tremors and trials, I still believe ours is a meaningful world. Blazing orange skies speak of it, wailing seals sing of it, I hear it whispered in the sea and the sky and the shore. And while we may feel like jigsaw puzzles thrown in the air, or wonder who we are and why we're here, the one who made the heavens and the seas made *us* by his infinite wisdom too.

The same hands that made the galaxies crafted us in the womb,[3] making us as significant as the stars.

I follow a slim, twisty trail over Lindisfarne's dunes through swaying, knee-high marram grass and imagine Cuthbert on this path with his hands outstretched, pushing back Britain's darkness with his prayers. After cutting through the fields, I head toward the village, find a bench by the harbor, and sit.

A fishing boat comes in to dock, the *whoomph-whoomph* of its engine rhythmic. Some eider ducks fly over. The castle stands majestic. The shore this side of the island is made of a million sun-bleached pebbles that clink and rattle in the waves.

My soul is at peace. My mind is at rest.

It's been a while since I've felt this.

I try to imagine Holy Island in Cuthbert's time, when it was just a simple wooden church and a few thatched dwellings, a school, a refectory, and some farms. I picture Cuthbert and his monks going about their daily work, crossing those mudflats to heal and preach, living to a rhythm of mission and retreat like the ebb and flow of the tides.

Lindisfarne was well established when Cuthbert arrived, founded earlier by a missionary named Aidan. A humble soul with a common touch, Aidan was known as a friend of the poor. He declined an offer to live in the prestigious royal fortress. He used what little money he had to buy and free slaves. When a king gave him a horse, he gave it away to the first beggar he saw, baffling the ruler to no end.

"Why would you give a royal horse to a pauper?" the king said, thinking it a waste.

"Is that horse more dear to you than a child of God?" Aidan replied. He knew that the beggar had divine worth, however lowly his status.

The king soon fell to his knees in repentance.[4]

And this is the wonder I must grasp before chasing any new calling: that while in comparison to the cosmos I am the tiniest of pebbles, a mere flicker on the timeline of history, the one who keeps those galaxies spinning wades through the stars to find me each day, counts the hairs on my head, watches as I work and rest, and holds me with a love that is beyond comprehension.[5]

The finest of earthly love we've felt is but a twig next to his Jupiter-size affection. A single leaf to a rustling forest. A mere microbe to a mountain. A faint candle to a galaxy's worth of suns. And until I dwell in this—dwell in a love that reaches beyond all measure, stretching higher and deeper and wider than I can imagine[6]—until I rest in this reality and let this love define me, I will forever seek my worth in lesser things.

"See what great love the Father has lavished on us . . ."

That I should call you a child of God.[7]

My Father.

My child.

My ultimate identity.

But is this identity enough for you?

I think of all the Me's I've wanted to be over the years, and the Me's I've been able to become. Being an author and broadcaster is a fine identity—as is being a builder, artist, mother, teacher, or something else altogether. But only one remains when the rest are stripped away. Only one can withstand the tremors of the world.

Can I be content as a child of God, before any career-based identity?

The truth is, I'm not sure.

⌒

The tide has ebbed, the road is still wet, and a taxi from Berwick approaches. It drives along the causeway onto the island and winds along its dune-rimmed edge before turning up the hill, entering the village, and stopping at the Manor House Hotel. I walk out to meet it.

There's a quote on the wall of the pub next door that seems apt for what's ahead: "Fishermen know that the sea is dangerous and the storm terrible," van Gogh said, "but they have never found these dangers sufficient to keep them ashore."[8]

A guy around my age gets out of the taxi. He has dark hair, a blue cap, and a heavy-duty rucksack on his shoulder.

"Hey, Sheridan!" he says as the car pulls away.

"DJ!" I say to my friend.

A man hug follows with slaps on the back. After dinner, we look over the maps. My retreat has been good; now an adventure awaits. It's time for stillness to make way for action. Because Durham beckons, the Lindisfarne Gospels call.

Tomorrow our pilgrimage begins.

CHAPTER 3

CAVES AND CROSSROADS

My hands are freezing. My trousers are soaked. The pelting rain sounds like popping corn under the hood of my raincoat. Droplets run along my eyebrows and drip from my nose, but shaking them off is futile. I glance at DJ, and we both break a smile. Sunshine is overrated anyway.

When the alarm rang early, I had peeked through the curtain to find a misty morning with rabbits grazing on the lawn. But the downpour had begun the same time the rabbits had scattered—the moment we left the front door. Now we plod along the causeway that winds beside the dunes, stepping aside for passing cars.

"Sleep well?" DJ asks.

I wipe the rain from my face and think before I answer.

DJ and I first met while working on a radio project tackling child poverty. We had visited developing countries together, discovered some shared interests, and enjoyed long conversations about life and God. DJ had moved his family to Aberdeen from Australia soon after Merryn and I came to Oxford, allowing some shared holidays to follow. In him I'd found a wise, fun, and empathetic friend. But . . .

"I forgot that you snore," I say as kindly as I can.

I hadn't slept all night. Not a wink. It isn't the best way to start a long hike.

DJ quickly apologizes, and we agree our cost-saving plan to bunk in the same room will need to be revised. I don't tell him that Merryn says I snore too.

We round a bend and reach the tip of the island. The dunes fall away, exposing the full force of the wind. It wraps our hoods around our heads, flattens our jackets across our chests, and turns those raindrops into liquid needles. With heads down and faces stinging, we head for the mainland, our adrenaline pumping.

We march along the causeway for forty minutes, the asphalt awash in sand from the receding tide, then head southwest on the mainland. The terrain starts to rise as we move into the countryside, the rain easing now but the path springy. We lean forward as we climb, our boots sinking under the load of our packs.

"Now our preparation is tested!" DJ says.

We'd done practice walks for months to prepare for the pilgrimage—DJ roaming the glens near his home in rural Scotland, and me trekking around Oxford. I had walked to St. Margaret's church in Binsey with its ancient healing well, and to St. Michael's in Cumnor to enjoy its quiet nave, up to Boars Hill where the bluebells flower, and across town to find C. S. Lewis's grave. Hopefully these miles have readied our limbs for the coming days. We'll find out soon enough.

Even if they haven't, I think those preparatory walks have accomplished much already. In heading out to the ancient wells and bluebell woods, I had left the confines of my fussing mind for unexplored roads and new vistas. Each walk had coaxed me out of myself and into its own small adventure.

A left turn. A right. Around the corner, straight on.

Walk on, Sheridan. With movement comes discovery.

We zigzag up the hill, walking the seams of patchwork fields, squelching in the soggy ground and picking blackberries from the brambles. The sun comes out; our jackets come off. Enjoyment masks my tiredness.

"Maybe Cuthbert walked this path," I say. The idea fills me with wonder.

Cuthbert was a solitary soul. He would sneak out at night to pray alone in the fields (or the sea, if one legend can be believed). When Hobthrush got too noisy, he built a shack on a remote island farther down the coast. There he communed with God, fought the devil, and counseled any who braved the seas to reach him. When he was later recalled to Lindisfarne to become its bishop, he left that beloved shack in tears.

So it's surprising to find that this introverted monk was also a man of adventure. He journeyed into the hills where warring tribes fought. He went to impoverished villages others avoided. And as he opened his Bible and preached in those places, he saw the lame walk and multitudes respond. Though happiest at home, Cuthbert would step out and follow God into the unknown.

"I think it's this way," I say, pointing up and to our left. We climb a stile over a fence and head toward a forest.

We're a few days into autumn—a season of falling petals, yellowing leaves, and seeds bedding in for the spring, but also of grand migration in the natural world. Right now arctic terns are leaving these regions for cooler climes down south, humpback whales are departing the Antarctic for warmer waters north, wildebeest are crossing the Serengeti plains for Kenya's greener pastures, and monarch butterflies are flapping their pretty wings across North America to Mexico. Wing to wing and head to tail they go, crossing earth and sea on their own pilgrimages.

We reach the top of the hill, enter a large open field, and take a right at the wooden sign pointing to our first stop.

A lesson from my twenties comes to mind as we walk. Seeking direction for my life, I had prayed for guidance, but a whole two years later I still had no idea what to do. Then some words from the Gospels had struck me with unusual effect. Keep asking, they said. Keep seeking and knocking. Because those who ask, receive; those who seek, find; and doors open for those who knock.[1] And that's when the hole in my strategy had been shown: I had prayed without seeking and asked without knocking, waiting for an epiphany instead of tapping on some doors. Once I put action behind my prayer by writing letters and making calls, my path into radio had become clear.

I take another step on that spongy track and feel this lesson reawakened in my bones.

There is no discovery without movement, no direction without action.

Ask, seek, knock.
Move.

⌒

The path takes us over the ridge, down the hill, through another gate, and into the woods. We wind down the slope through the scrub between the trees, circle around into a clearing, and look up. On the underside of the mountain is a dark cavern spanned by a large sandstone ledge the size of a small shopping center. Dark and deep, it looks like a giant eye peeking from the earth.

"There it is," DJ says.

"Wow," I say.

We have arrived at Cuthbert's Cave.

We walk up and look inside. The cave is high enough for us to stand upright with room to shelter a couple of dozen people. Its dark walls are cold and damp and graffiti-etched with names and dates going back to the 1700s. There's moss on the floor, a sodden fire pit at the entrance, and a peaty smell in the air. I sit down on one of the cave's large rocks, take off my boots, and rummage through my pack for chocolate.

Out of the way and hidden in the hills, this is a place Cuthbert would have loved. One legend even suggests this was his base for a time. But while the history is sketchy, another scenario seems more likely: that Cuthbert came here in his coffin.

The image we have of the barbarous Vikings can be traced back to Lindisfarne. One June day in 793, Norwegian raiders attacked it with ferocity. Ships with dragon heads and oars like wings! The monks had seen nothing like them. Bodies slain in the priory; the monks' blood poured on the altar! It was history-making brutality.

More raids followed over the next eight decades, and in 875 the surviving monks fled. They put the Lindisfarne Gospels and some relics in Cuthbert's coffin and walked the flats. For the next seven years, they were fugitives. This cave was their first hiding place.

"It's eleven o'clock," DJ says. "That walk took longer than I expected."

I rub my left heel through my sock. My feet are sore sooner than I predicted.

With miles to go we don't rest for long. DJ readies the map for the next leg of the trip, slips it into its plastic sleeve, and hangs it around his neck. We wind back through the trees, up and over the cave, and head southeast. The little white way-marks dotting the track should get us to our next stop fine.

We walk along the forest edge dwarfed by pines ten times our size, their boughs swaying, their limbs waving, their needles aflutter and alive. After twenty minutes awash in the calm of their rustling, DJ stops and looks around.

"Do you think we missed a turn?" he says, looking puzzled.

It does seem a while since our last waymark. We look over the map and try to find our place, correlating circles and squares with our surroundings. Deciding a left was needed about ten minutes back, we reluctantly turn around.

Those monks walked over a thousand miles on their seven-year trek, pushing Cuthbert's coffin by cart over the hills and dales of north England and southern Scotland. They walked this way and that, occasionally in circles, and sometimes straight toward enemy ground. Homeless and restless those arduous years, I wonder if they ever regretted leaving the island, or beat themselves up for taking a wrong turn, or wavered over the way forward, given the peril around them.

I'd heard echoes of such anxiety in my readers, some of whom were at major crossroads in their lives. One woman had to decide if an untried medical treatment was worth the toll on her body. One man was about to risk his savings on a move to Europe in hope of a better life for his family. "We have waited seven years to adopt," another woman told me, "and I can't endure this much longer. But if we give up now, will we regret it later—always wondering what might have been?"

It was a weighty choice for each of them, because:

The operation may not work . . .

I may not find a job . . .

The adoption agency might still call . . .

Things might all go wrong.

And as I've read these words and the angst they've carried, reviewed my own journey, and prayed for something helpful to say, it's seemed to me a more secret fear has lurked behind each worry:

That our lives will be ruined if we don't make the perfect choice.

Merryn and I had felt this. Maybe I still do now. But if I've learned anything from our infertility ordeal it's that only God knows the end of every possible journey; we must choose a path and find out in time. Better to pray, seek counsel, make a choice, and walk forward, trusting God to correct any wrong turns we make, than forever rue our decisions and wonder what might have been.[2]

"This still doesn't feel right," DJ says, stopping again. We're back to the big tree we thought was our turning point, but the track down the hill seems to head the wrong way. With my chocolate hit gone and my energy ebbing, I have to force myself to focus on the map.

"That square there," I say, pointing to the page. "Is that the shed on the hill?"

"Or is it the barn over there?" DJ says, nodding across the field.

"If it is, then this circle must be our tree."

And suddenly all the symbols and contour lines start to make sense, and we realize we're not where we ought to be. We look at each other and groan, then laugh, then start back up the hill.

We had been on the right path all along.

———

"What about your childhood, Sheridan? Was it a happy one?"

We walk along the hilltops now, over canola crests and barley slopes, on rutted lanes and bridleways, ever watching for the next waymark. The sky is gray and we have occasional rain, but the undulating land lifts the mood.

"I was safe, I was loved," I reply. "But I was a lonely kid too."

Dad and I once found an old go-cart at the dump. We fixed it up with new wheels and fresh paint, and, with Dad standing on the corner watching out for cars, I would rush that cart down our driveway, turn a quick left and a right, and race joy-fully down the street. Mum would make me banana milkshakes after school, sew up costumes for drama class, and take me on train trips during the holidays. Dinners were shared around the family table, and in the evening we watched *Mork and Mindy* or *CHiPs*. On weekends I'd take Bliff the dog on my dragster bike and we'd ride over the hills feeling free and curious. Only once did I find my home life deficient.

"I was seven years old and decided I'd had enough," I tell DJ with a smile. "So I packed some socks in a little basket and left home."

"How far did you get?"

"About halfway up the street."

"What brought you back?"

"I wanted an ice cream sandwich, the kind Mum made with wafers. I called out from the driveway, asking if she'd bring one down."

"And?"

"Mum said she'd make me one if I came back inside."

DJ laughs. "Gotcha."

"It was a subtle trick, and I fell for it."

With a father who fixed carts and a mother who fixed treats, my childhood was as secure as one needed. The school-yard, however, was another matter.

For whatever reason, I found it hard to make friends. Perhaps it was being an only child until I was twelve, while the other kids had siblings to play with. Or the English accent I'd picked up from my parents while the others spoke an Australian drawl. Or the fact I was in a weird religious sect at the time, or that I was useless at sports in a sports-mad town. I was shy, lanky, and spent lunchtimes alone, always the last one picked for the team and the first to drop the ball.

"When I was ten I had a friend named Richard who used to come over and play. But in grade six he got in with the rough kids and started bullying me instead. He'd follow me around throwing stones and calling me names."

"How long did that go on?"

"With him, not that long. Someone said I should challenge him to a fight and get it done with. So I confronted him one morning."

"And you won?"

"No, I got pulped. All the kids talked about for the rest of the day was how Richard jabbed me left and right while I just flailed around."

DJ winces.

"Oh well. Richard later became a boxer and competed in the Olympics, so I like to think I helped him find his vocation."

We laugh, and that's good. To laugh at pain is to transcend it. But those days held a terror that's hard to forget. With bullies at the gate, the world seemed sinister.

"I was off of school once with the flu, but the dread I felt was worse than the sickness. Remember those trays under our desks that held our pencils and things? I had this fear that while I was at home the kids were rummaging through my stuff, looting what they could. Sure enough, when I opened my tray the next day I found the pencils broken, my ruler snapped, the pens used, and my highlighters gone. The kids all smirked. I nearly burst into tears. I felt violated, worthless . . . and completely alone."

We pass some paddocks and stables and tall wooden sheds stacked high with hay bales and pause to pat a friendly mare that's ambled to the fence. A waymark points to a tree-lined track. We turn and head toward it.

"What was your childhood like, then?" I ask.

In contrast to my suburban lot, DJ's early years were spent in the country—on a four-thousand-acre property farming angora goats for fleece. He grew up catching crayfish in the creek, hunting wild rabbits and dingoes, and watching sunsets over the fields from the top of his favorite tree.

"It was primitive living, though," he says with a laugh. "We were too far out to be on the electricity grid, so we had this old wartime generator for power. When it broke down, which happened a lot, we'd huddle around a black-and-white TV perched on the kitchen stove that Dad hooked up to a car battery. The battery always ran out before the end of the movie! We used kerosene lamps for light, our hot water came from an old, tin wood-chip heater, and our phone was an old Bakelite thing with a crank you turned to get an operator."

It sounded like a tale from the Depression era, not the 1980s.

"Money was tight. We generally ate well from the farm— pumpkins, watermelons, and the goats' meat too—but some dinners were just bread and homemade jam, as that's all we had. Once or twice Mum even boiled up stinging nettles for our greens!"

I hadn't known this history. Walking with someone helps to tease out their story.

"That was just living meagerly, though. Our real problems came from the neighbors, who were *rough*. They seemed friendly for the most part, but our tools and livestock were always going missing. They ultimately drove us off the land."

"What happened?"

"Dad was walking around the property one morning when he came across a bloodbath. Scores of our most valuable goats had been shot. Some had been dragged away; others lay there mauled. We'd lost thousands of dollars' worth of stock, which we couldn't afford to replace. When the local policeman came around, he was physically sick at the sight. But while all the evidence pointed to the neighbors, it seemed to get swept under the carpet. It was a small community, so everyone knew what happened. The kids on the bus even bragged about knowing who did it."

Now it was my turn to wince.

"I tried hiding a tape recorder in my bag to catch what they said. It didn't work, but I guess it was my way of trying to help my parents. Drought, hard times, then this—it all put a strain on their marriage. I'd lie in bed at night hearing them argue. We never did recover financially. A little while later we sold the farm and moved back to town."

"How old were you when this happened?"

"About nine."

I shake my head and breathe out deeply.

"That's a lot for a kid to deal with."

"I remember standing in the schoolyard feeling so sad at the injustice of it all," he says, glancing at me briefly before his eyes turn to the ground. "And that no one else in the world knew just how sad I felt."

Our boots crunch on the gravel. Wind wisps through the pines. We step from mottled shadows into open sky, with cows grazing the plains and a scent of wheat in the air. We plod quietly for a while.

"How did that experience shape you?" I ask finally.

DJ looks ahead for a moment, thoughtful.

"You know, it was Mal Garvin who showed me just how much it had."

A pioneer in the Christian world, Mal had touched millions of Australians through his radio programs and community projects and had been a leading light for many of us.

"One day I was telling him how passionate I was about children living in poverty in developing countries. Mal asked me why I was so drawn to help children, and why specifically children in poverty. At first I couldn't answer, but the more he probed the more my answers spiraled back to the farm."

"Where you'd once lived hand-to-mouth," I say.

"And felt the pain of injustice and vulnerability as a child."

It was an effect I could see at work in my own story. Prone to befriend those who stood alone at parties and draw out the quietest voices in discussions, my sensitivity to the lonely and left out no doubt went back to my school days. Those ransacked trays and lunchtimes alone had given me a heart for people on the fringes.

"Those hard times shaped my passions," DJ says.

"They helped fashion who you became," I add.

It's a marvel when you think about it: all the taunts and trials of our childhood years becoming the soil from which our best selves can grow.

⸻

We're on the descent now, a lush valley in view. Sheep munch the slopes, a river wriggles below, and each stile and gate steps us down to the tidy town of Belford.

"I met myself as a teenager once," I say to DJ. "Saw him standing right there in front of me as a seventeen-year-old boy."

The surreal experience happened one June afternoon. One moment, I was sitting in my living room; the next, I was in a nightclub back in 1989 staring at teenage me. He wore a white shirt and torn jeans, Converse sneakers, and his hair long and wavy. He stood before two turntables and hundreds of people, a shy boy in a DJ competition about to face humiliation or glory.

I had relived the moment many times in my memory but now watched it unfold in detail. Seventeen-year-old me started his seven-minute set, mixing one song into another, then cutting into a third. The crowd responded well, but they couldn't see what I did: all the hopes and insecurities inside that kid, how his heart beat fast and his shaking hands sweated, how he hoped this night would make him significant.

"It was a video," I tell DJ. "Someone had uploaded the competition online. I found it by chance and watched it, stunned. It was footage of me I'd never seen."

Slowly we make our way down the mountain, the skies changing from gray to white to the lightest powder blue.

"That contest sounds like a defining moment for you," DJ says.

"It was, but I didn't know what I was getting myself into."

My stomach had begun to knot the night the competition's organizers brought us entrants together for a meeting. I had walked in and found the room full of big-name DJs with serious talent. There they stood with their Adidas shoes and their caps turned backward, fresh out of their nightclub gigs and their music videos. And there I was with my Duran Duran haircut, fresh out of my bedroom.

"I was in over my head. I started planning to pull out."

"But you didn't?" DJ says.

"I don't remember how it happened, but at some point I decided to go ahead, face the challenge. I bought new records, worked on some new tricks, practiced my set over and over each day, and made it onto that stage shaking in my shoes."

"How did you do?"

"I cut the power to a turntable halfway through." I laugh. "Apart from that, my set went fine. I didn't win a place, but that didn't matter. I had taken my first big risk and survived. It felt like crossing a threshold of some kind."

We veer right then take a left, where our feet touch cement. After hours of gravel and grass, it feels strange. Stone-brick Belford has some stores and a post office, a pub and an old shop selling handmade toys. We decide to stop for a drink and a rest.

Later in that video, the one I'd found in June, the camera zooms past the dancing masses and settles on a figure up the back in the shadows. I can tell it's me before my face is in view. And right there as I watch I want to reach in from the future and tell that seventeen-year-old a few things: that he's searching for God without realizing it, and God will soon make the first move; that his life will take an unforeseen turn because of this, and this turn will be for his good.

And I want to tell him that the fear he felt and the step he took in spite of it is a pattern he can expect for anything in life worth having.

Face the fear. Take the risk. Don't run away.

Good things can come when you step into uncertainty.

We climb a tall, grassy dune to the top. Sea breeze rushes our faces. Waves crash, seagulls squawk and hover. A castle glows orange in the setting sun. We have made it to Bamburgh, the small coastal town where we'll lodge tonight. Its majestic castle, perched on an eight-acre rock ledge 180 feet high, fills the sky with towers and turrets.

We can see for miles up here, even back to where we've come from. To our left in the distance we spot the slim terrain of Lindisfarne, where the morning storms whipped our backs and pushed us into the day. Behind us lie the hills and woods with their winding paths and secret caves; and before us, just a mile offshore, lies the tiny isle where Cuthbert pitched his shack and lived in blessed seclusion.

Tomorrow we head right, following the sands south—making wrong turns, no doubt; perhaps getting some cuts and abrasions. And maybe the wrong turns will just be part of moving forward, and the abrasions part of us becoming ourselves. And maybe, like all our journeys, great discoveries will be made simply through our moving.

Because it's easy to stagnate when life goes wrong—to withdraw into the past or hide in one's room. But there are new paths to tread, new ventures to pursue.

Go somewhere new.

Walk on.

CHAPTER 4

VISIONS AND WHISPERS

A nd will that be two eggs each, or three?" he asks.

DJ and I sit at a long oak table, pots of homemade jam ready before us. The table sags, the rugs are worn, stairs creak, and windows rattle. My bed was in the attic, my mattress was lumpy, and a famous revolt was once hatched in this very room.

The seventeenth-century farmhouse that housed us last night is both family residence and bed-and-breakfast. It also happens to be where the Jacobite rebellion of 1715 was plotted to get a Catholic king back on the throne. The fact our randomly chosen lodging has a place in the nation's history books adds a nice detail to the day.

The mattress may have been lumpy but I've woken refreshed, albeit with stiffer joints than I expected this early in the trip. Breakfast gets served a little later in the country, so when the clock strikes 8:00 a.m., DJ and I are more than ready for the steaming plates of bacon and eggs Charles, our host, slides before us.

"Where to today, then?" he asks as we dig in.

"Our first stop is Beadnell," DJ says, "then we're on to Craster."

"That's definitely a three-egg trip," Charles says, smiling.

"We're following the life of St. Cuthbert," I add between mouthfuls.

"Well, then, you'll want to spend some time next door."

———

I click the iron latch and push the heavy door. Even at this time of day, the church is open. Inside it's cool and quiet, the aroma one of old wood and hymnal paper. Early light filters through the stained-glass windows, warming the gray stone walls and dark wood pews. A table in the nave celebrates the fruits of harvest—sheaves of wheat, baskets of apples, carrots, melons, tomatoes—and beyond it a single lit candle glows in the chancel. We step softly.

Before founding Lindisfarne, Cuthbert's predecessor, Aidan, built this church—or at least a wood and thatch precursor to it. A piece of that original building is said to be grafted into this twelfth-century replacement. I walk to the baptismal font and look up. There hangs a thick timber beam, darkened by time, serving no structural purpose. It fits the ancient accounts, so who knows?

I tour the church by its windows. Etched with saints and angels, kings and crosses, their animated figures contrast with the static pillars of stone. I pause at the rear window. A kaleidoscope of color, it depicts a lamb being tended by Frideswide, patron saint of Oxford, and a teenage Cuthbert roaming the hills with a shepherd's staff.

I pass through an archway and enter the chancel. A silver cross stands center on the backlit altar, and behind it statues of northern saints like Cedd, Chad, Finan, and Hilda look out. I move toward the candle. It hangs by a chain inside a simple shrine. An engraved sign nearby explains its significance: in 651, St. Aidan, founder of Lindisfarne, missionary to the English, died near this spot, or somewhere close by.

People queue to view the room in which Francis of Assisi passed away or pay to see where Thomas Becket died in Canterbury Cathedral. But there are no buses here, no tourist lines. It's just us in an unlocked country church and a small, flickering flame.

The place of a monk's passing would rarely fascinate me either. But this spot is significant because, according to the scribes, something special happened the night Aidan died. They say a stream of light pierced the darkness and shone on this spot. They say angels traveled down it to carry the saint's spirit home. And they say this vision transformed a teenage boy tending sheep in the faraway hills, who on seeing it was gripped by a divine claim on his soul.

In the morning he traded his shepherd's staff for a place in a monastery.

A man of God in the making.

Cuthbert had received his calling.

We pull the gate closed and step into the street, leave the farmhouse behind and the quaint homes of the village. Towers and turrets again fill the sky, we pass yesterday's mount with its view for miles, and a pencil-thin track leads us through the dunes to the wide shore of Bamburgh Beach. The tide is out, the damp sand firm. We head south under a white-rimmed cloud toward a glowing blue horizon.

"Tell me about a turning point in your life," I say to DJ as we settle into stride, "a time when you clearly experienced God's guidance."

DJ has a thumb tucked under a strap of his pack while his other hand works a trekking pole. He looks into the distance, reflective.

"Joining the band was one of those moments," he says.

Capable at school and musically gifted, DJ spent his adolescence in sports, singing in garage bands, performing in school musicals, and keeping his social calendar full. An atheist from his early teens, he considered God unnecessary—until one night when he found himself with no place to go.

"I suddenly felt the isolation of my atheism," he says, "that I was completely alone in the universe. Without the constant parties and distractions, life was empty."

"And that got you searching?"

A thick plate of cloud hovers high above us, its gray bulk casting a blue hue on the sand and its distant edges white and luminous.

"Friends had been inviting me to church for months, so I finally went. I liked their ethic of justice and caring for others, and I started reading the Bible myself. But, and this might surprise you, when I first read the Gospels, I didn't like Jesus much."

Even secular people like Jesus, so this *is* a surprise.

"Calling himself '*the* way' and '*the* truth,' 'the bread of life,' 'the light of the world'—it all sounded a bit arrogant to me. I mentioned this to a friend and he agreed that it could be seen as arrogant—unless it was true. And if it was true, it wouldn't be arrogant.

"The pastor of the church used to give altar calls at the end of his sermons, inviting anyone who wanted to become a Christian to step forward. No one ever did. Then one day I found myself walking to the altar in front of everyone. I still wasn't sure if God existed, but if he did, I wanted to lead the kind of compassionate life I was hearing about. So I prayed, 'God, if you are real, I want to live your way.'"

"That's beautiful," I say.

"And from that Sunday on, the altar calls stopped. It turned out I was the only unbeliever in the church and they'd all been aimed at me!"

We laugh as the dawn becomes morning, as seagulls begin to soar, as our legs march in unison. A few locals are out now, mere dots in the distance, their statures tiny in contrast to the vast sands and high cloud.

"A few months later," DJ continues, "a band called the Travelers came to town. They were a Christian group that toured full-time, performing in schools and jails and doing big concerts. There could've been five hundred of us at their show that night. And as I stood in the audience watching them perform, a sudden, overwhelming sense hit me:

"This is what you're going to do.

"I didn't hear a voice as such, and I didn't have the language to understand it as a calling. It was more a deep sense of *knowing*. And it went beyond any aspiration I had, as I didn't think I was anywhere near good enough to play in a band like that.

I started wondering what the experience meant when I felt something else:

"You're going to join this band.

"I started to shake. It all felt crazy. What was I supposed to do now—go and tell them to give me a job? And just as all this was running through my head, the band's manager came to the mic and said the band was looking for new members for next year's tour, and if anyone was interested, to come and get an application form."

I laugh.

"I was so nervous queuing for the form I nearly went home a dozen times. And I was pretty sure my audition tape would be rejected. But I was accepted. It was the beginning of over five years of full-time touring with them and other bands."

We round a point and feel a sudden blast from a powerful westerly wind. A couple of dogs start barking. We brace ourselves and lean in. Raw and rushing, the breeze lifts dry sand from the dunes and shoots it across the firm, tan beach. Ribbons of white begin swirling around us like jets of light charging to the sea. They dash and swerve like dancing spirits. Like holy gusts. Like ghostly currents.

We push into these sandy streams, breaking their flow as rocks do rivers, and as we cross a peninsula to another beach, I think of my own first turning point.

I was a shy kid used to playing on his own, then an introverted teen drawn to solitary pursuits. Standing on a stage was the last thing I'd aimed to do, whether before a conference crowd or a radio audience. That I was ill-fitted for such a career seemed sure after my first attempt at public speaking.

"It was a friend's wedding," I tell DJ with a little embarrassment. "I'd been asked to MC the reception, which was dominated by the bride's large, rather dour family. I stood up, welcomed everyone, and started with some lighthearted jokes. But no one laughed."

DJ closes his eyes and groans.

"I grew more nervous and started fumbling my words. I got little more than blank stares and a few polite chuckles the whole evening. I went home feeling embarrassed and exposed, and vowed never to speak in public again."

"Well, that vow certainly got broken."

It's an irony for sure, one I rarely forget. And the U-turn came after finding faith and praying those two years for some life direction.

"During a church service one night," I say, "they played a video about a large radio network sharing the love of God overseas. As I watched, my heart began to pound."

"Were you interested in radio then?" DJ asks.

"Not at all, which is why the experience was so surprising. The following week I wrote to the Australian office of a similar network, knocking on the door, I guess, to see what it might all mean. I knew I needed both Bible and radio training, and I asked if they offered anything like that there.

"It took two weeks to get their reply, and during that time something strange happened. Over the following days, two persistent thoughts circled my mind:

"*Make contact with the Bible College of Queensland.*

"*Get in touch with Family Radio.*

"I didn't know much about the college. Perhaps someone had mentioned it to me somewhere. But I had heard of Family

Radio. It was a small, amateurish station back then, and, well . . ."

"It wasn't an attractive option for you," DJ offers.

"Right. And yet, gently, persistently, those two thoughts kept coming:

"Bible College of Queensland.

"Family Radio.

"A letter arrived from the network's director. He explained that they were just a two-person fund-raising office, so they couldn't offer me any radio or Bible training. And then he said, 'But if I were you—'"

DJ smiles, knowing what's coming.

"'I would make contact with the Bible College of Queensland—'"

"And," DJ adds, "get in touch with Family Radio."

It was an experience that would set the course of my life for the next eighteen years—putting me before both radio and conference audiences, doing the very thing I'd vowed never to do.

I pick up a stick to use as a makeshift walking pole and recall other stories of direct guidance I've heard. A husband and wife I know were once walking in the woods, praying about whether they should go to Vietnam as missionaries. Suddenly, a child with a toy gun jumped out from behind a tree, pretending to be a soldier. "Anyone for Vietnam?" he said, before running off to his friends. The couple went to Vietnam.

Another couple I know were thinking of starting a church in a deprived area of Oxford. One night the wife had a dream in which a girl from the area appeared and said, "We're hungry, and if you don't feed us, nobody else will." The couple started their church, and that girl became a Christian.

I know a woman who was told by a stranger: "God wants to use you to bring healing to others and to write a book about your experiences." Several months later, visiting South Africa on business, she was told exactly the same thing by someone else she'd never met. She's now praying for others' healing and writing her book.

Sometimes the God of wonders guides us with clear words and lights in the sky. Like a rushing wind that blows wherever it pleases,[1] he sweeps us into his plans and into unexpected places.

———

Van Gogh leads us into a starry blue night. Da Vinci takes us to the Last Supper's table. Monet guides us to a lily-filled pond, and Rembrandt to the scene of a prodigal returning home. Dickens takes us through old London's streets, Harper Lee through the segregated South. Perhaps at its heart, all art is pilgrimage—a trek to a sacred somewhere through a frame or a page. Perhaps every song is a journey through a lyrical landscape, every beat a step forward into new territory.

I feel this now as we shuffle off the beach and onto a hard dirt path, as harbor boats lift and tilt to the rhythm of the waves and our rubber soles thump the earth in four-four time, a kick and a snare in our own pilgrim-song.

We cut through the village of Seahouses then follow St. Oswald's Way, a marked trail honoring the Northumbrian king of Cuthbert's time. It was Oswald who first invited missionaries into this region, paving the way for Aidan's arrival.

Aidan's calling was different from Cuthbert's. We find no

angelic visions in his story, no heavenly voices or pounding chests. Oswald's request was first met by another monk, whose evangelistic attempts failed miserably.[2] When the mission to the English seemed over before it had begun, Aidan stepped in to try again. While Cuthbert was called through a dramatic sign, Aidan simply followed an opportunity.

"I guess that describes my becoming a youth pastor," I say as we tread on. "An opportunity taken. Not that it lasted long."

As clear as my calling had been and as prepared as Bible college made me, when graduation came, no doors to radio opened. What did open was a position for a youth worker at a church an hour away. Though I had little experience leading students, the church took a chance on me. I wasted little time when I arrived.

"I pulled a team together and started youth-focused church services. We did big social events on weekends and got the kids into midweek prayer groups. I had goals, mission statements, strategies, and growth plans. I was more seeker-friendly than Bill Hybels and more purpose-driven than Rick Warren."

DJ laughs.

And good things came of it. Over the following months the youth ministry grew rapidly, students came to faith, a brilliant team of leaders emerged. The kids were happy, their parents were happy, the church leadership was happy . . .

"But I was falling apart."

I was a morning person working evenings and struggling to sleep. I was learning on the job, and the learning curve was steep. The same months of growth saw their fair share of crisis—a boy left paraplegic from a tragic accident, a girl dragged through a custody battle by her divorcing parents, kids in

trouble with police, leaders slipping up morally. On one occa-
sion a parent took my words badly, locked himself in a room,
and threatened to never come out.

"Pastors deal with problems all the time, but I wasn't ready
for this. The experience revealed some personal flaws in me,
too—an unhealthy sense of responsibility for others, a fear of
letting people down, always feeling like I hadn't done enough
or done it right. I slipped into insomnia, which spiraled into
depression. Eighteen months later, I handed in my resignation."

DJ shakes his head, feeling my words.

"And you know what the worst part was?" I add. "The sheer
confusion of it all. Was this Satan disrupting fruitful work, or
was it God moving me on? Was I abandoning my post when
things got tough, or discovering what I wasn't suited for? I had no
dreams or impressions or prophecies from strangers. I prayed,
consulted others, and decided to leave—often wondering if I'd
made the right choice."

We enter Beadnell and sit down on a bench by a gravel
beach. A tradesman sits in his van with a newspaper on the
dash and lunch in his hands. Still full from breakfast, we need
little more than an apple. We refold the map and trace the journey ahead.

The dotted line on that page winds through Beadnell's
streets, past family homes and holiday shacks, back south toward
the dunes, then through a large caravan park of on-site cabins.
Moving on, when we enter the park we pass dozens of those
square white dwellings, a treeless acre of PVC cladding, the clean,
straight lines of their prefab frames a contrast to the contours
of the coastline.

"Your experience leaving the church reminds me of my

application to Oxford," DJ says, "and everything that came after it."

DJ had come to England to pursue a PhD in theology. Oxford University seemed like the perfect option, and after months of preparation, his entry into one of the world's most competitive establishments looked assured.

"Meeting with faculty, being told my topic was strong, having a key theologian agree to supervise me, having you two nearby—everything seemed set to fall into place."

"All the signs pointed in the right direction," I say, remembering the time.

"And then they said no." There's confusion in his voice, even now.

The disappointment had been deep for DJ and his wife, Louise. They loved Oxford, had chosen a church to attend, and had started planning where to live. Thinking they were watching God's plans unfold, they were left bewildered by the closed door. A fog seemed to descend on them for months afterward.

"And yet," I add, "look what followed."

What followed was a move to Scotland and a place at Aberdeen University, a home in the village of Kintore with its small, welcoming community, and arguably the best school in the country for their daughter's special needs right at the end of their street.

"We couldn't have ended up in a better place," he says.

A swing gate leads us back into dunes, over grassy peaks and rutted slopes. We veer and dip along the jagged coast, cross a river, then take a fork in the road. How many times have I drawn straight lines in my mind between a goal and its fulfillment, from where I am to where I've wanted to go? But there are few straight lines in the natural world. It's all bend and kink and curve.

"What happened after you left the church?" DJ asks.

"I could say that growth happened, as I worked through the personal flaws those turbulent months revealed. I could say wisdom happened, the lessons learned from that short season proving vital for the years ahead. I could say discovery happened, as I came to understand where my gifts really lay. But in the short term, what followed was something more surprising: I got a radio job—almost the moment I left."

This turn of events raised new questions, of course. What had that church job been about? For a time my straight-line thinking saw it as a diversion from my real calling, a detour off the freeway to radio. But maybe it wasn't a detour but a destination in itself, the first stop on a longer, winding journey. Maybe the path of one's calling is more a forest walk than a freeway.

Whatever it was, I see something now that I haven't seen before—something that gives my current angst perspective:

When all I felt was confusion, I was still being led.

When I couldn't hear God's voice, I was still in his hands.

———

We know how Cuthbert's calling worked out. After his angelic vision he trained at a monastery in Melrose, served at a sister house in Ripon, and then returned to Melrose as prior. He spent twelve years leading Lindisfarne, eighteen years as a hermit, two years as a bishop, then his final months in solitude. Interestingly, only one of these career moves is described as being supernaturally directed.[3] Cuthbert had moments of clear guidance but then followed the path wherever it led.

Whether a novice, prior, hermit, or bishop, the essence of his calling remained the same—Cuthbert was a missionary monk, a churchman to his dying day. Things haven't been quite so straightforward for DJ or me.

"When did you start feeling drawn to academia?" I ask, swinging my stick at the grass fronds drooping across our path.

I knew part of the answer lay in DJ's own experience of burnout. Five years as a touring musician exacted a toll, the long drives, late nights, and physical demands leading to a physical breakdown. Taking time out to study was part of his recovery.

"I wasn't filling time, though," he says. "I was full of questions about my faith and hungry to learn, and this was my opportunity to do it. Theology became my favorite topic, and lectures on God became moments of worship for me. This passion was reflected in my results, and one day the dean suggested I take my studies further."

"What about music, though," I prompt, "after the clear calling you had?"

We round a bend and follow a waymark to the left, where another narrow path leads us up a rise like a crease on the contours of a hand.

"There's a garden at the entrance to Disneyland in California," DJ says, prefacing his answer with a backstory. "It has a giant face of Mickey Mouse made of flowers. It's a nice garden, a great place to pause and take photos, but it's only when you go beyond it that you discover the real joys of Disneyland itself. When I realized I'd need extra time away from music to recover, this picture came very clearly to mind. It was like God was saying the 'garden' I'd been in had been good, but there was much more for me beyond it. Music was just a part of who he'd made me to be—"

"But he had more in store for you," I say.

"And it was time for me to discover it."

The path leads up the hill; the crest opens to a vista. We stop to take it in. A white beach below us sweeps around to a sandy point, and beyond it another shore arcs and sharpens to a peninsula. It's a giant's-eye view of cascading coastline. People inch along the sand, as small as poppy seeds. A ruined castle stands on the distant cape, a solitary feature between the silver sea and sky.

"Do you miss being on radio?" DJ asks as we head down the slope.

"Almost every day," I reply, my voice softening and a twinge of loss pinging in my chest. After a pause, I try gathering up the reasons why.

"There's nothing quite like a compelling hour on live radio," I add, "talking to a politician one moment, an author the next, having a musician perform and a board full of callers lined up, never knowing what tricky question you'll be asked or what's going to be said, knowing that what you discuss will shape lives, maybe even change them, and that you have only seven seconds to hit the Dump button and salvage the show if something goes wrong. I miss that—the thrilling, risky magic of it all. I miss sitting nervously in the chair as the intro music plays, miss cracking the mic switch on in that first anxious moment, miss the conversations that follow . . . miss doing something I know I did well."

I probably miss the affirmation that comes from a public

role, too, not that I'd want to admit it. Whatever else I miss, it's surely tucked inside the ball of sadness I feel growing in my gut. Maybe I should change the topic.

"The question I face now is whether to go back to radio or focus on writing instead."

"What does Merryn think?" DJ prompts.

I give a short chuckle because the answer is easy. For all my romanticizing of radio, it's an intense business, too—there's always another story to hunt, topic to follow, interview to prepare, or debate to track as the next show looms. Merryn had watched it claim all the energy I had and believed now it was writing's turn for time. I had truths that needed sharing.

And I have noticed something since coming to the UK— that I'm being sought out more for my own ideas. With the broadcaster's hat on, I was a facilitator of others' stories; with it off, I am a speaker with my own insights to share. Moving back into the host's seat could jeopardize that.

"Maybe I'm the last one to get that the season is changing," I concede, smiling.

We walk on down the hill and along the beach, with fingers under our straps and trekking poles swinging, as the wind picks up and the path bends and twists.

Silence falls between us, a rare moment without words. And in that space I reflect.

What is the work of your heart? I find myself asking. *What does your soul long to do?*

What is the yearning within that won't go away, the passion that rises whenever you pray, the persistent desire, proven by time, prompted by love, full of life, that peacefully calls and beckons? What is the whisper you hear when you're still within, the Yes *you can give your energies to? What is the dream that hovers like mist?*

Deep down, Sheridan, what do you want *to do?*

I want to craft words that captivate the heart and open eyes to see God. And I want to write *these words before I speak them.*

Maybe there's more for me to discover beyond that first calling. And maybe I really am the last one to get it.

Because some callings come as visions in the night, with hovering angels and lights in the sky, while others appear as open doors, opportunities for us to step into. But many start as a whisper in the heart, perhaps confirmed by a letter or the words of a stranger, but a desire no less that cannot be escaped—authored by one who moves us to will and to act according to his good purposes.[4]

Onward we walk, the castle growing larger, the marram grass swaying, the wild wind rushing.

CHAPTER 5

CASTLES AND ASHES

The castle dominates our view for the rest of the afternoon, its turrets flat against the sky like a storefront in a Hollywood set. We walk back into the dunes with the sea on our left, the fortress slowly growing larger. It stands high on the horizon like a city on a hill, like a kingdom of old, a majestic ruin. A golf course leads to it like a royal carpet. We wind through its bunkers and greens.

We reach a headland. A ridge of sheer cliffs curves around to our left and a wall of grassy slope stretches out to our right. We skirt the slope for several minutes then climb the bank and look up. Before us stand two giant stone towers—the great gatehouse of Dunstanburgh Castle. DJ walks toward its large arched entrance while I stop to read the information board.

No one quite knows why Thomas, Earl of Lancaster, built this place. Constructed in the fourteenth century, the castle wasn't near any major settlements or military sites of the time. Second in wealth to the king, Thomas had other lavish properties to enjoy. There's little evidence he even lived here. With history lacking, clues to its purpose must be sought elsewhere—particularly in its design.

Dunstanburgh Castle was quite the sight in its day. Its grand gatehouse would have instilled awe in all who approached it, and artificial lakes fed by underground channels created spectacular reflections of its soaring towers. Positioned on that lofty hill, its Camelot-like splendor could be seen for miles. And this is where we might grasp its role. The castle was for Thomas what a private jet is for some today—a symbol of elevated status, a sign of his importance in the world.

It's an impressive legacy when you think about it. Seven centuries on, Dunstanburgh Castle keeps Thomas's name alive. But the tribute is mixed. On that information board I read he is also remembered as an "arrogant and unpopular" man.

We head down the slope against a line of visitors, each one stopping at the board. And for the rest of the afternoon I think of the earl, who enshrined his life in bricks and gained a heart of stone.

We reach Craster by late afternoon. The small village is famous for the kipper, and its smokehouse cooks the herring delicacy in oak barrels, wafting a smoky-savory scent into the air. Our lodging is just out of town. We've walked fourteen miles, and my feet are sore. When we arrive I sigh in relief to find a deep bath in my room.

I run the bath and sit on the floor, waiting for the tub to fill, and stare at the tap without reason or focus, my brain in neutral, hazed by tiredness.

Must charge my phone.

Should try the kippers.

Gosh, my feet do hurt.

And out of this blur a memory surfaces of an encounter I had with a friend.

Chelsea and I had been colleagues once, before she'd moved to England, and when Merryn and I arrived in the country she'd invited us around for a meal. She would collect us from the bus stop, she said. We were to look for her *black BMW*.

Chelsea had taken us on a tour of her neighborhood, and what a place it was. She'd shown us the *prestigious* college all the politicians attended, the *exclusive* street where her mothers' group met, the *selective* school where her daughters were enrolled, and the *famous* gallery now owned by *her* friend. Here was the *specialist* salon where her nails got polished. There was her favorite café. If we had more time we'd drop in for a latté. It was where all the *celebrities* went.

After driving us past *Madonna's* favorite bar and her husband's *high-end* law firm, we had arrived at Chelsea's nice-but-average home in the more affordable part of town. Do sit down, Chelsea said, on the *Italian* couch. Did we like the new kitchen? It was *German*. She'd had the light fittings imported from *Spain*. And had she mentioned the dining table was *handmade*?

On it went, one association after another, like a bowerbird adorning her nest with shiny things. But Chelsea's attempts to impress only pushed us away. Her façade of success hid who she really was and left her indifferent to her guests. All the sticks and bottle tops made a finely woven nest so thick it formed a cocoon.

I swish the water in the bath. A dash of cold is needed. Replacing my clothes with a towel around my waist, I sit on the rim and lower each foot in. And as I watch the waterline rise, an image of a man comes to mind.

He is sitting by a window in a hotel room, his chosen location for our interview. His attractive face is known to many, a fact somehow echoed in his countenance. A dutiful assistant brings him a drink. Time is short; must keep this brief. I review my notes and check my levels, then begin to record.

The interview started well, I recall. My guest had a powerful story, full of fears faced and obstacles conquered. But I couldn't shake the feeling something lurked behind our interaction. A passing comment soon brought it to the fore.

"You are inspiring thousands of people," I said between questions.

"Not thousands," he muttered under his breath. "*Millions.*"

And with a shake of his head as if pitying my ignorance, he put me straight on his credentials. He had visited a dozen countries *this year alone*, speaking to *tens of thousands* of people each time. He'd been on the *covers of magazines* and on the *biggest TV shows*, reaching *hundreds of millions* more. Through his preaching he'd seen *the lame walk*, *the deaf hear*, and *many thousands* find a place in heaven. And with words I'll never forget, he then added this: "Stop anyone in the street and they'll probably know who I am."

Arrogant, I think as I lower my body into the tub. *Pompous.*

Few character traits are more hideous than an excessive belief in one's own importance.

The choppy waters settle as I lay still in the bath, its warmth going to work on my sore limbs. And soon the water becomes a mirror that reflects the tiles of the wall the way Dunstanburgh's lakes once reflected its towers.

One more memory floats in, of a conversation with Merryn that happened just after our coming to England. It stings on recollection.

"I've noticed something," she said, "that you might want to keep in check."

"What?" I replied, growing concerned.

And Merryn told me that when people asked what I did for a job it wasn't long before I laid out my own credentials—how I once hosted a *national* radio show with *thousands* of listeners, interviewing lots of *well-known* guests.

"It sounds a bit—"

"Desperate?" I said, feeling ashamed.

"No," she said, "just insecure. You don't feel confident in who you are right now, so you recount your last accomplishment to feel significant."

Feeling professionally bare through the loss of my role, I had allowed my inner bowerbird to go to work. With string in beak and bottle top in claw, it had woven a cover out of yesterday's achievement in an attempt to hide its nakedness.

I sink beneath the bath's surface. Water spills to the floor. The tile towers tumble in the rippling waves.

Tack up a façade of success. Thread on shiny symbols. But if God is who he says he is to me, and I am who he says I am to him, neither will help or be necessary.

———

My Father.
My child.
Let the implication of this penetrate, Sheridan: you are accepted, valued, and significant already.

Let all the strings and bottle tops wash away.

———

"What were we doing five years ago?" I ask, as DJ and I walk a tree-lined road in the early light, the taste of smoked fish on our tongues. The song of birds and a dry-stone wall running beside us give the morning a particularly English feel.

Just a mile away is the home of Charles Grey, better known as Earl Grey, the nineteenth-century prime minister known for the famous blend of tea. He had the brew specially made to suit the lime-heavy water of his well, but through a lack of business sense never made a penny from it.

The whole Grey clan sounds wonderfully unconventional. One countess carved the gargoyles in the family church but never got around to finishing them; another commissioned the church's altar paintings, which, the family admits, were never a success.[1] One descendant found Lord Grey's tomb so ghastly he took to it with a hammer and chisel. Here's to British eccentricity.

"Five years ago," DJ reflects, "I was exploring PhD opportunities."

"And I was reducing my radio hours to write more," I say, noting how our current aspirations have been years in the making.

"It makes you wonder where we'll be in five years' time," DJ adds.

"Or even a decade from now."

The ragged stone wall leads us back to the coast, to whinstone cliffs and limestone shores covered in shingle. Each pebble here was first a rock, and before that a mountain, and before that magma, and once the dust of stars. Each has been fashioned through a thousand small collisions into its own unique form.

"I read a story about Alfred Nobel once," DJ says, following a new thought.

"The Peace Prize guy?"

"Yeah, but here's the thing: while we associate Nobel with peace, his career was largely one of war."

With a father who invented the naval mine and did early work on the torpedo, it was perhaps only a matter of time before Alfred's own chemical experiments led to similar inventions. And they did—most notably, dynamite. Unlike Earl Grey, however, Alfred amassed a fortune from his creations. By the end of his life he held hundreds of patents for explosives and ran dozens of armament factories. Alfred Nobel became one of the world's leading merchants of weapons.

"Alfred's death was announced by a French newspaper one day," DJ says, "and it carried a scathing obituary, accusing Alfred of growing rich on inventions that kill. The headline was brutal. It read, 'The Merchant of Death is Dead.'

"But Alfred wasn't dead. The newspaper had mistaken him for his brother. And this bizarre event got Alfred thinking about how he'd be remembered."

The path Alfred chose to tidy up his name was unexpected, not least for his family. When he did die a few years later, they were shocked to find he'd left most of his wealth to establish a prize for the betterment of humanity.

"No one remembers Alfred as a merchant of death today," DJ adds, "but rather as the man behind the leading peace prize of our time."

Our road begins to bend inland, so we step onto a dirt path along the cliff. And as we trace the precipice I consider what a gift Nobel's mistaken obituary was.

Because each of us is a mist, a breath, the spark of a struck match: present for just a moment, then gone.[2] And facing this fact gets us serious about our living. Alfred Nobel got to glimpse his legacy early, see the impression his life would leave, and adjust it accordingly. Consulting your death shows you how to live and reveals what's most important to you.

"Few of us get to read our obituaries," DJ says. "But we do get to shape our legacies by what we give our lives to now."

And what will your legacy be, Sheridan? I wonder as we walk. *Which of your efforts will live on after you?*

I know what my legacy won't be, and that's children. I have some idea what I'd like it to be, and that's a book of mine staying in print for years to come. But what *will* it be?

I'm not sure I can answer with any certainty. And I wonder if that's a problem.

———

Along the cliffs we go, across a bridge, through fields, and into another small village where a stout man with bushy gray hair loading crates on a tractor waves a friendly hello. His yard is a mountain of colorful lobster pots, a mass of frames and nets stacked three meters high. I stop to ask for a photo, and we get talking.

His name is Main, a third-generation fisherman who has worked these waters all his life. One of the last to use the traditional coble boat—a flat-bottom, high-bow descendant of the Viking long ship designed for the rough North Sea—he catches salmon in winter, lobster in summer, and is proud of this row of homes being one of the few genuine fishing villages left in England.

"Where yair headin'?" he asks in his thick northern accent.

"To Durham," I say, "to see the Lindisfarne Gospels."

"I haird they're beau-iful. And did yair see the ol' house at Howick?"

DJ and I look at each other, unsure.

"You'd have past it a couple mile back. No walls or nowt, just an excavation site. They found remains of a settlement there goin' back ten thousand years, like."

Absorbed in conversation, DJ and I had walked past one of the oldest traces of human habitation in Britain—the remnants of a Stone Age hut dating to 7800 BC.

The age is staggering. Before there were alphabets, calendars, wheels, or pyramids; before Petra, Stonehenge, the Colosseum, or Acropolis; before Abraham left Ur, Moses left Egypt, Solomon built his temple, or Jerusalem had walls, a fur-clad family gathered by a hearth in a tepee-like hut up the road.

"It gives yair mind a wobble just thinkin' 'bout it."

We give Main our word we'll "speak nowt" about his village. "Don't want them Londoners comin' up and openin' their fancy cafés," he says, smiling. Within minutes of our farewell its homes and cobles are out of view.

The day is bright, the morning's rays pushing through diaphanous cloud to fill every crevice. Soft shadows follow us, feather edged and feather light.

"What will you regret not doing before you die?" I ask DJ.

Mortality is on my mind. If DJ doesn't like this solemn shift in conversation, he has only his obituary stories to blame.

His eyebrows rise at the question, then compress in thought. "I'll have to ponder that for a bit," he says. "All I can think of are platitudes."

"Give me the platitudes," I say, "and the rest may follow."

"Well," he says, "I'd regret not completing my PhD. Or not being a good husband. Or not seeing my girls grow up healthy and happy . . ." And here he pauses, the question going to work. Like a diver probing the depths, he has sighted a first treasure.

"I would regret," he says slowly, "not giving my daughters a strong foundation for their lives—not helping them meet God for themselves and discover their vocations, or setting them up as best as I can to meet the challenges they'll face. This will be more complex with Bethany, of course."

Bethany is DJ's eldest, a six-year-old sunburst of blonde hair and big smiles who also has cerebral palsy. DJ and Louise foresee caring for her the rest of their lives.

"She still prays for you and Merryn every night," DJ adds.

"And I still sing the Flying Hedgehog song," I reply.

Maybe any success Merryn and I have will be due to that little girl's prayers. And maybe that soft toy will always whiz through the air to the tune Bethany and I made.

———

"As for a career," he says, "I'm still trying to figure that out."

Having spent the last few years at a nonprofit organization working to alleviate child poverty—a good fit given his early experiences—DJ finds that his job back in Australia is looking uncertain. The company has treated him well—keeping his role open while he completes his PhD here, even helping to fund his studies—but a recent restructure means his position may not exist on his return.

"Maybe that's a good thing," he says. "I wouldn't want to return to life as normal. I've grown through my studies. I've changed."

"Then what would you regret not at least trying?" I prompt.

"I'd like to publish my thesis when it's done," he says. "And I'd like to do more academic research. I'd regret not pursuing those things at least." And then the diver stretches out his hand and touches something more.

"I would regret," he says thoughtfully, "not taking every opportunity, however large or small, to become a teaching theologian of the highest standard I could reach. And I think *teaching* is the key word. As much as I'd regret not publishing my work or doing further research, my real drive is to train others for their life and calling, helping them discover the wonder of knowing God more deeply."

"Writing papers won't be enough for you," I say. "You need to lecture too."

And with that, another treasure falls into the diver's bag.

"That's it," he says, the discovery coming clear. "I would regret not becoming the teacher that is in me to be."

"What about you?" DJ asks. "What would you regret not doing?"

We reach another caravan park, all clean lines and right angles. Cutting through it would save us time, but efficiency isn't important today. The shingle shore is now sand again. We step on it and take the longer route around a peninsula.

"I'd regret not getting a puppy," I say.

We laugh but it's true—Merryn's and my desire for canine company is currently frustrated by an escape-ready broken fence our neighbor has yet to fix.

"There are book projects I'd regret not pursuing," I say, speaking each thought as it comes. "I'd regret not doing more with my photography too—I have hundreds of images on my laptop benefiting no one. And I'd love to make a documentary one day. I think I'd regret not giving that door a push."

The tide is out, leaving a wide, empty beach at the end of the peninsula. We head for firmer ground near the water's edge, the damp, compressed sand absorbing our steps. I wait for the diver to swim deep.

"I would regret not building lifelong bonds with a few close friends," I say.

With our Australian connections now a world away, it's something I'm conscious of. Distance will test those historic bonds, while friendships in England will take time to form. And with kids out of the picture, I think of Merryn's and my future. It may be the hands of those friends that lay us in our graves.

We walk our muted steps on that wide expanse of beach, my answers to the question coming more slowly than expected. I wonder why more hasn't surfaced.

Regret, Sheridan, I prod. *What would you truly* regret *not trying? What opportunity is within your reach to pursue?*

74

And a thought begins to form: words, feelings, images.

"There are certain points along life's path," I say, "when even the most secular person starts looking for a spiritual guide."

"Uh-huh," DJ says.

"A few might seek a religious leader at those times, but most will turn elsewhere—to columnists, TED speakers, authors of self-help books, and the like."

"Right," he says.

"We have many good preachers speaking in our churches," I add, "but fewer good communicators speaking to the world."

"That's true."

"So here is what I'd regret," I say, spotting a glint on the ocean bed. "I would regret not doing what I could to become a guide to the spiritually curious—as they travel to work with their radios on, or sit in their cafés with a book in their hands, or read their columns or stream their videos. I would regret not becoming a voice of faith to the mainstream world through media, stage, and bookshop shelf, offering a God-given word at those turning points."

I find my words awkward to speak and embarrassing to hear, inviting as much self-scorn as they do excitement. *What, you? Settle down, lad. You're not that clever.*

I guess a vision is always a vulnerable thing to share.

"Am I capable of doing something like that?" I say. "I don't know. I even doubt it. But a decade from now I'd like to have moved toward that goal. I'd sure regret not trying to."

———

An hour on gets us to Alnmouth, a quaint town of flower boxes, tearooms, and colorful terrace homes. We rest by the red telephone box on the main street, then head downhill and cross a bridge before finding our footpath end at a major road.

"This seems the only way forward," DJ says, checking the map.

The road is narrow and hemmed by hedges, leaving little room to avoid traffic. Seeing no other option, we walk on single file.

A car soon pulls up behind us. We lean into the hedge to let it pass, our packs suddenly feeling wide. An oncoming van rushes around the bend, breaking heavily when its driver sees us. A motorbike swerves past us, barely slowing down. A car toots its horn. A truck rumbles by.

"We need to get off this road," I say, feeling trouble loom.

We pick up our pace. It's a third of a mile before we find a break in the hedge with a small barbed wire fence. We swing our bags over, stretch the bottom wire, and slide underneath into a lush private farm of grazing Suffolk sheep.

"I hope the owner doesn't mind," DJ says as we start treading the field.

"If he does, just tell him we've come to talk religion."

And we chuckle at the thought of a tough northern farmer running off in terror, his boots kicking up mud and his hands in the air. After ten minutes of trespassing, a new public path appears, and we never do get to try the line.

"I interviewed Tony Campolo once," I say, referring to the American sociologist and church leader. "He suggested doing this exercise: Imagine your life is over and you're lying in the casket at your funeral. People have gathered around, and they're talking about you. What do you hope they're saying? What are your family, friends, colleagues, neighbors, and people around the world remembering of you? Tony suggested we write these things down and ask ourselves every day if we're becoming the kind of person others can say such things about."[3]

"Sounds like a challenging exercise," DJ says.

"And a revealing one."

Because when I imagine such a scene, of either myself or someone else, I don't hear those gathered discussing much of what we judge our lives by. I don't hear them talking about the universities we attended, or the degrees we received, or the positions we reached in our firms. Our awards won't matter, or the sales goals we hit, or how pretty or fashionable we were. Italian couches and BMWs won't get a mention. Or being known in the street. Or having a radio show.

"If Merryn is at my funeral," I say, "it won't be my books she remembers. And my nephews and nieces won't reminisce about my career. Neighbors may not see any documentary I make, and being a 'voice of faith' may not matter much to friends."

"I can't imagine my thesis getting mentioned at my funeral," DJ says.

"As important as that thesis is."

There are few trees on this stretch of path and the sun is breaking through the clouds. I take off my hat to wipe my brow.

"It's not that our work won't matter in the end," I add.

"It just won't matter most," DJ says.

When God first placed humanity on earth, he made us coworkers in his world-crafting enterprise.[4] So we can expect to develop ambitions to farm land or build homes, raise children or design clothes, do business, make art, tend animals, teach classes, write books, do theology, or trawl the seas in coble boats.

But when our dearest gather by our caskets that day, our

achievements won't be first on their lips. Instead, they'll recount a few shared tales—the time we hitchhiked home without a dollar in our pockets, or got an audience with Bono, or lost that crazy bet—before another kind of memory will emerge:

"He always made me laugh . . ."

"She showed me what I could achieve . . ."

"When no one seemed to care, he listened . . ."

"I was sick and she visited me . . ."

"I was ashamed and he forgave me . . ."

Memories not of careers but of the kind of people we became.

What qualities will our mourners recall? I wonder. That we were kind, compassionate, generous, courageous? That we were reconcilers, truth tellers, peacemakers? Will Merryn be able to say that I loved her well? Will nephews and nieces remember a playful uncle? Will colleagues say farewell to someone who cared for them, not just success? Few tears will fall for a builder of castles.

Solomon built his temple. Esther saved her people. Paul took the gospel across the globe. But for every biblical story celebrating heroic achievement, there are a dozen passages more calling us to simply be godly. And in a culture like ours that measures worth by fame, perhaps we miss the significance of this.

Because a kind word in a cold world can melt sorrow and bring a tear to the eye. And a compassionate act in an indifferent age can interrupt despair. Empathy can restart a lonely man's story. A word of truth can let a captive fly free. Forgiveness can jam the wheel of reprisal. Grace can heal wounds. Goodness can overcome evil. This is good news for those who've lost the dream. Because when we can't become who we want to be, we can still become who we're *meant* to be:

Be holy, because I am holy.[5]

Have a heart of flesh, not of stone.

⌣

Cuthbert left an impressive legacy. By the time he died at fifty-three, he'd seeded the gospel into England's bloodied soil and seen thousands of Christians flower. He'd united a church on the verge of schism,[6] and his wildlife laws were even the start of modern conservation.[7] The Lindisfarne Gospels would be crafted in his honor; he'd become a saint, have churches built in his name, and a whole city—with a stunning cathedral at its heart—would rise on the site of his shrine. Cuthbert's short life would set much in motion. Pilgrims would even walk in his steps.

We enter our next town via a tree-lined road, passing more flower boxes and quaint terrace homes while another majestic ruin grows in view. Warkworth Castle is smaller than Dunstanburgh but older and in better shape. We skirt the base and reach the castle gates. Its great tower is in the shape of a Greek cross.

"There's a vulnerability to our legacies," I say, as we walk by the moat.

We step onto the road, our shadows sharp and dark now from the stark afternoon light. We head downhill, then follow the river out of Warkworth.

"How do you mean?" DJ asks.

"Few of us will get an obituary in the papers," I say. "And those who do will have their story told through another's eyes."

"That's true," he says.

"And who really knows what people will say at our funerals," I add. "The memories they have may be different from what we imagine."

DJ nods.

"The work we've done will be passed on to others—whether a farm, a book, or the ideas in your thesis—and it will be up to them how much our work lives on."

A stone wall runs beside us. Birds sing. The river flows.

"What people remember of us may not be the whole story," I conclude.

That's certainly the case for Earl Grey, the prime minister we remember for tea, not for signing Britain's historic antislavery laws into action. And our memories of Alfred Nobel may be even more flawed. Despite the prod of that mistaken obituary, Nobel continued making weapons to his dying day—a fact at odds with his stated pacifism. Perhaps he hoped the weapons he made would ultimately bring an end to war. Or perhaps his Peace Prize was simply an attempt to have a more positive reputation. We'll never know.

"I guess our lives are only ever fully known to God," I say.

"And our legacies are ultimately up to him," DJ says, "not us."

There's a story told about Cuthbert that's one of my favorites. It describes a time he went to comfort survivors after a plague had ravaged the region. Accompanied by a priest, he visited each town, offering Scripture, prayer, and a listening ear.

In one village Cuthbert prayed for everyone he could find. "Could there be anyone left for us to help?" he wondered, keen to miss no one before leaving. The priest took another look around—and found someone.

A woman stood at a distance, clutching a child to her chest.

Her cheeks were wet for a son already lost, and the child she now held was nearing death.

Cuthbert approached her, took the boy in his arms, and prayed, blessed, and kissed him. "Do not fear or be sorrowful," he told the woman, "for your child shall be healed and no one else of your household will die." And the boy lived.[8]

Books in his honor. Churches in his name. A city built on his shrine. But perhaps eternity will record Cuthbert's legacy more like this:

A mother noticed.

A body held.

A forehead kissed.

Holiness.

CHAPTER 6

RIVERS AND STREAMS

I wake early and watch the dawn prize a crack between the sea and sky to let the first light in. Another simple room, this time in a harborside guesthouse in Amble. A pine table in the corner holds a cup and kettle. I rub my eyes, open a sachet of coffee, and take my steaming mug back to bed as the crack becomes a glow.

Sunrise stillness. Daybreak quiet. Hope seems tangible at this twilight hour before the world is roused to its angst and ambitions. My feet feel tender, but I feel light. *Just be present. Walk on.* Something in me is changing. I have more answers to find, but I'm learning.

I shower, then meet DJ in the small dining room downstairs for breakfast. After repacking my bag with half-dry clothes hung on the radiator, I head to DJ's room for prayer. We've been reading a psalm before walking each day, but this morning we turn to Cuthbert's favorite gospel, John, instead. "I am the true grapevine," Jesus says there, "and my Father is the gardener." The Father lops off each branch that dies through unbelief, and prunes the fruitful ones to be even more productive.[1]

It's funny how a verse you've read for years can speak to you afresh. It's the *fruitful* branch that God prunes, I note, and this is to make it *even more* fruitful.

He snips each stem of yesterday's success to prepare us for a brand-new season.

The start of day four sees us back on the beach, on sand swept clean by last night's tide and dogs frolicking in its puddles. Soft clouds hang above. A lighthouse stands in the distance. The receding water has cut finger-wide tributaries into the sand that twist like roots in search of moisture.

We get about a mile into the day before DJ motions to stop. My heels already hurt, and I've noticed him rolling one foot. He sits down to remove his left boot, revealing two adhesive bandages on his sole and a third blister starting to form.

This beach is our pilgrim's way all morning, our solitary tracks in the virgin sand slowly joined by others as the sun climbs. For the first time on the trip, breakfast has been basic. When our stomachs start bubbling, we leave the shore in search of food.

A beachside road leads to a junction with some homes and a village hall. We look around for a supermarket, but there isn't even a corner store. All we find is a small ice cream shop. It has a sign out front saying "Cresswell Ices" and a chalkboard listing today's flavors. I can see jars of sweets inside and an old peg-letter price board on the wall. There's a crate of used novels by the door and a dish of water out for pets. A man and woman sit at a table outside. They greet us as we approach.

"Is there a pub nearby," I ask, "or somewhere else we can buy lunch?"

The woman wears a burgundy top and her gray-streaked hair in a bun. The guy wears a denim shirt and a worn cap. "The nearest pub would have to be the Plough," he says, looking to the woman for confirmation.

"Aye," she says, "in Ellington. That's the closest shops too."

"There's nothing south?" DJ asks, finding Ellington is west on the map.

"Not before Newbiggin," she says kindly.

We drop our packs to relieve our feet and decide an ice cream is better than a detour. As we walk inside the woman follows. It turns out she's the proprietor.

Brenda bought this shop some years ago, she tells us, after just a few hours' training in ice cream making. The rough-built shelves on the wall hold toys as well as treats—dominoes, jig-saw puzzles, snakes-and-ladders games—and a handwritten sign offers instant coffee cheap. This is an unpretentious enterprise with its own charm. We take chocolate and vanilla cones back to the table.

The guy in the denim shirt is John, a regular who tells us the region was built on mining. "But things got tough when the mines started closing in the eighties."

"There isn't much work in the area now," Brenda says, sitting back down. "We get holiday makers in the high season, which helps, but the village is mainly retirees. The kids have to move away to find jobs."

"How many people live here?" I ask.

"There are ninety-seven of us," Brenda says. "Oh no, I lie. It's ninety-six now since ol' Joe passed away on Wednesday."

A villager stops in to say hello, his Labrador lapping at the water bowl. As he leaves, Brenda tells us how much she enjoys life in Cresswell.

"It's peaceful here," she says, "and the people are friendly. I love running the shop: talking with customers and watching the children's faces when I hand them their ice creams. People seem to enjoy coming in for a coffee and a chat."

"I can see that," I say, as a couple approach and greet Brenda by name.

"Make people feel welcome," she says, "and they return."

John asks what brings us north and we tell him about our pilgrimage. A few minutes later the postman arrives, and he and Brenda trade village news. When John leaves he gives Brenda a hug before he goes. I marvel at the warmth of this close-knit community built around ice cream cones.

"There's nothing too special about the place, really," Brenda says. "It's just home." A home where everyone is known by name and visitors get a warm welcome.

Two children rush inside and tap the refrigerator glass above the choc-chip tub, and as DJ and I leave Brenda to her work, I think of my own last visit home.

It was just a few weeks ago, a speaking event in Australia allowing a quick trip to my hometown, Brisbane. Keen to see the city at night, I'd driven to a cliff called Kangaroo Point that overlooks the central business area. And as I sat watching the cars rush along Riverside Drive and the lights shimmer on the river that winds through the city, I realized I could see many of the spots where my life had taken shape.

Tucked among those high-rise buildings was the club where I'd competed as a DJ. To my right was the Story Bridge, which Dad had driven me across each day to my first job out of school. On my left was Southbank Parklands, where Merryn and I had our first date and where we'd returned the night I proposed. Farther up the river was my first flat, and the college I attended, and the first radio station I worked at.

"But the strange thing was," I tell DJ as we start down the path, "despite all these memories, Brisbane didn't feel like home. And it never had."

We pass the holiday park that helps Cresswell stay afloat in the high season, its cabins and caravans full of residents far from their own hometowns.

"It wasn't until we moved to Sydney that I felt a sense of home."

"Why do you think that was?" DJ asks.

I had pondered that before, wondering how the city where I'd spent twenty-six years of my life could evoke less affection than one I enjoyed only five.

"I guess home is about belonging," I suggest. "It's the place where you feel comfortable being you. In Brisbane I felt like a books-and-ideas man in a beer-and-football town. But in Sydney I wasn't alone in liking art galleries or writers' festivals, and dropping a theological word into a conversation didn't kill the mood."

DJ smiles.

Sydney had stretched me too. Its cosmopolitan mix of cultures and lifestyles forced new questions on my faith that made it grow, and the professional opportunities it brought expanded my skills. Sydney became the place where my career dreams flowered. It felt like the best possible place for me to serve the world.

"Maybe home isn't just about belonging," I add, "but about becoming. It's where you're free to be who you are, and also become who you're meant to be."

"What about Oxford?" he says. "Could that become home now?"

I think of Oxford's Bodleian Library with its twelve million books, many of them stored in tunnels beneath the city center—making it a town literally built on ideas. I think of Oxford's sandstone spires that glow orange at dusk, and its lovely misty mornings. I think of the book I've written and its unexpected fruit—a direct result of our moving there. Oxford's culture and its beauty sit well with this soul, and it's stretching me to become someone new.

But as Oxford is a town of academic elites, there are only so many conversations this amateur can join. And I've had more greetings from strangers on Detroit's streets than from some of my own neighbors. I'm still finding my place in Oxford's church scene, and working from home can get lonely. I'm an Australian among the English and feeling like neither. I've a little way to go to fully belong.

"When the bus pulls into Oxford and I see Magdalen Tower and people punting on the river and narrow boats on the Thames," I say, "I feel grateful to live where I do. But will Oxford become home the same way Sydney did?"

We pass the villager we met earlier, his Labrador now running off the leash.

"I don't know."

The wind picks up on the road out of Cresswell, tousling the grassy sandbanks and making white noise rush in our ears. We haven't knowingly met any other pilgrims yet, but we have met a few hikers. One approaches us now, his curly fringe swaying and walking stick swinging. We trade hellos as he passes by.

"You know what's been coming to me as we walk?" DJ says. "The difference between deep and shallow community."

"How do you mean?"

"We've met some nice people these last few days," he says. "Friendly fishermen, kind villagers, the hikers we've swapped tips and directions with along the way. But none of our conversations with those people has gone very deep."

It's true. In many cases we hadn't even shared names.

"Now contrast that to what's happening here," he says, his hand motioning between us. "We're not just walking the same path but sharing the joys and trials of the journey—the history, the wrong turns, the scenery."

"The blisters," I add.

"And not just that but we're talking about our childhoods, our hopes, our regrets. You can't get that personal with someone you've just met, of course, but it does make me wonder how deep some of our other relationships in life go."

"When we never get past superficial talk," I say.

"We cross paths and share tips," he says, holding his cap down against the breeze, "but never really share our lives."

Cuthbert knew this deeper kind of community, but only with a few. One such friend was Elfleda, a princess-turned-nun at a nearby monastery in Whitby. While it was Elfleda who sought Cuthbert for counsel, he seemed equally comfortable entrusting her with his own secrets. Cuthbert told no one but Elfleda how he believed his final years would unfold, a confidence she kept for years.[2]

Another companion was Herbert, an island-dwelling hermit with whom Cuthbert enjoyed a special bond. Living far apart, they met just once a year for mutual encouragement. When Cuthbert revealed that his health was failing, Herbert fell at his feet in tears. "We have served God together on earth," he said. "Ask God now that we may depart together too." Cuthbert prayed and Herbert got his wish. The two friends later died on the same day on their respective islands.[3]

But perhaps Cuthbert was closer to no one more than to Boisil. One of Aidan's first monks, Boisil was the one who welcomed Cuthbert into the monastery after his angelic vision. It was Boisil who taught him to pray, heal, and preach in the hills. Boisil became Cuthbert's mentor, confessor, and father-in-the-faith. More than that, Boisil became what the Celts called an *anam cara*—Cuthbert's soul friend.

At the end of his life, Boisil called Cuthbert to his side. "I have only seven days left to enjoy my health," he prophesied. "Learn from me all you can while I'm able to teach you." When Cuthbert asked how best to use the time, Boisil suggested they read the gospel of John together. Over the course of the week Boisil instilled in Cuthbert a deep love for that book, foretold some key events in his future, then died having shaped his protégé profoundly.

"Some years ago I read an essay by the novelist Dorothy Sayers," I say as our footpath ends and we step onto a grass verge. "It was about how we view work, and it resonated with me so much."

"What was her idea?"

"That work isn't something we should do to live, but the thing we should live to do. Since humanity is made in God's image, and God makes things, we express our humanity best when we make things, too, through meaningful work."[4]

"There are lots of ideas about what it means to be made in God's image," DJ says, his theological mind engaging, "but I get her argument."

"Sayers was countering the idea that we work just to earn money. She saw the corrosive effects of that all around her in the 1940s: people living in drudgery, workers lacking interest in what they produced, factories spewing out poorly crafted goods just to keep up the economy. For her, work could be so much more. Its purpose wasn't just to pay the rent but to express our faculties. We should find worthy work to do, she said, and do it with excellence. She even longed for the day when strikes were held over not just pay and conditions but the value and beauty of a company's products."

"Imagine that." DJ chuckles.

"Sayers's point was that work should be fulfilling. It can express our God-given creativity, provide an outlet for our talents, and, as with God at creation, lead to the satisfaction of finding our efforts to be 'very good.'"

A gust of wind catches my visor, and I clutch my cap before it flies off.

"And all this spoke to you?"

"She helped me see that all careers could be callings from God," I say, repositioning my hat, "not just the 'religious' ones, and that every job should be done as an act of worship. I'd tasted the joy of doing work I felt gifted for, and this seemed a good way to choose a profession. I see now, though, there are weaknesses in the argument."

We round a bend out of the breeze's flow, the road ahead stretching into miles of treeless field. With few cars around, we start treading the asphalt.

"For Sayers, work is an essential part of our lives. It's what gives us meaning and significance. But there's a problem with that."

"Not everyone can work," DJ says.

"Exactly. What about the elderly, the unemployed, the chronically ill?"

"What about children?" he adds.

"Surely their lives have meaning and significance too. Work isn't the only way we express our humanity."

"Some don't get the option of doing work they're gifted for," DJ says. "People on the poverty line or with families to feed *have* to work to live."

"And how many careers have been dashed by a family crisis or a war," I add, "where the dream job is given up to do the duty at hand? We can't always do what we want to do, but doing what we *need* to carries its own honor."

These are largely theoretical critiques for DJ and me, given that neither of us face such situations. It's a further problem that has me uncomfortable.

"I read another essay recently," I say, "by an ethicist named Gilbert Meilaender, who raised more fundamental questions on this approach to vocation.[5] The live-to-work mantra is destined to fail us, he says, because it turns work into something it was never meant to be—a means of personal fulfillment."

When thinkers such as Martin Luther and William Perkins first taught that everyday work could be a calling, they said a calling had two main features: it was given by God, and it was done for the benefit of others.[6] Whether you were a farmer, preacher, painter, or housewife, obedience and service—not self-fulfillment—were the motivators for one's calling.

"If a sense of meaning or enjoyment came," I continue, "it was a happy by-product of a calling, not the focus of it."

"That's a different emphasis from what we have now," DJ notes.

"For many of us," I say, "work has become the dominant thing in our lives, the primary basis of our identity, the main way we seek significance."

Even for you, Sheridan.

And here lies my discomfort. For all my wrestling with Meilaender's essay—*Doesn't the purposelessness of unemployment prove that work is important? If we're suited to some jobs more than others, isn't fulfillment a sign we've found where we fit?*—I had to admit that work had come to play too great a part in my sense of self. I had established an identity as a writer, speaker, and broadcaster, then felt adrift when those roles were gone. Perhaps my hankering for a new calling now is really a sign of a deeper need—for a bigger picture of who I am.

I am a child of God.

And then you are more.

Road signs mark this as a seventy-mile-per-hour zone, but there are no cars around. We start walking along the faded center line, checking over our shoulders now and then for approaching traffic.

"According to Meilaender," I say, "we should pull work down from the high position we've given it and seek our fulfillment in other things."

"Like what?" DJ asks.

"Like friendship."

For the ancients, friendship, not work, was the great joy of life. "No one would choose to live without friends," Aristotle wrote, "even if he had all other goods."[7] "The heartfelt counsel of a friend," Solomon said, "is as sweet as perfume."[8] Each of us needs a comrade or two to know and be known by, to share the joys and trials of the journey with, to tell our stories to. And whatever our jobs, whether ill, unemployed, or elderly, we can be Elfledas, Herberts, and Boisils to others, too—hearing their secrets, bearing their tears, shaping and being shaped as we share holy things.

"I no longer call you slaves," Jesus went on to say in our gospel reading this morning, "because a master doesn't confide in his slaves. Now you are my friends."[9]

The idea is profound. To advertisers we are markets, to retailers we are consumers, to monarchs we are subjects, to governments we are voters, to businesses we are clients, to employers we are staff, but to the Master we are something else, something often seen as everyday and ordinary but now graced with divine status.

Not slaves or workers, and not just children of God. To us he gives the high and holy identity of *friend*.

———

The wind again picks up and the white noise whistles and industrial chimneys start appearing like pencil stubs in the distance. A smatter of raindrops patters across the asphalt. We pull on our raincoats before a shower falls.

———

The rain pips and snaps against our hoods as we settle into silent walking. And my thinking turns to a dinner I had with a couple not long ago.

"What do you do with your time, Coleen?" I'd asked the wife.

"Not much," she said, which I hadn't believed, so I asked about her week instead. My unbelief was proven justified. Coleen's last seven days had included spending the weekend helping at a large church conference (an event touching several hundred lives), devoting Monday to mentoring two young women, Wednesday and Thursday to helping a friend recover from surgery, plus cooking, cleaning, and caring for her family, and then offering hospitality to me that Friday night.

"'Not much?'" I said incredulously. "Coleen, you're doing a lot with your life."

"I don't always feel so," she replied, and I asked why.

"Because I'm not earning an income."

I think, too, of a story I read about the director Krzysztof Kieślowski. As he interviewed actors for one of his films, a young actress had told him how, when she felt sad, she'd walk the streets of Paris to be with people. A few years ago, on the verge of a breakdown, she'd done this and within moments caught sight of the famous mime artist Marcel Marceau, by then a very old man. The actress walked past him, then stopped and turned to give him another look. To her surprise, Marceau stopped and turned to look at her, too—then gave her a big smile lasting several seconds.

"He saved me then," the actress said.

And she and Kieślowski wondered whether Marceau had ever given a greater performance than saving a young actress with his smile.[10]

***

A third thought now, of an old lady I heard about. She tended a small grave in a Houston cemetery marked with a simple headstone that read "David."

"I found him as a discarded fetus," she said, "out back in the clinic's trash. I rescued that little body and gave him a name and a proper burial."

That was 1989. She'd tended that little gravesite ever since.

Puddles start to form on the asphalt's edges. Our boots flick water with every step. A Gypsy Cob mare stands placidly in the field—white body, pink nose, feathered legs like flared jeans. We wander over, and she welcomes our pats with a nuzzle and a batting of her fine eyelashes.

My book launch day, I remember, was planned to the detail—with interviews to do and reviews to read and posts to share on social media. When I wasn't on the phone or checking the best-seller list for a miracle, I scanned my e-mail. Around midday I got a message from a friend of ours named Tanya. It was her birthday that day, but all celebration had evaporated after a fight with her husband.

"So here I am," she wrote, "sitting in a library cubicle crying, longing to hide and wondering again what I'm on this planet for."

And in the rush of that day, as I paused to find words to comfort her, it struck me that a writer was not what Tanya needed then.

Terry lost his job, then broke up with his girlfriend. When I met him, he'd been living on the streets for a few weeks. Feeling prompted to help, I offered Terry our spare room. We had little experience taking in the homeless but we did have a bed, a phone, a shower, food—enough to help Terry get back on his feet.

He came down for breakfast the first morning. "I haven't slept that good in weeks," he said, freshly shaved and looking his twenty-eight years again. And as Terry ate his toast and planned his visit to the job center, he noticed our broken fence in the backyard. By that afternoon he was out with a hammer and drill, attempting a fix.

Terry was with us for two weeks, helping around the house when he wasn't looking for work. Not once did he hear me give a talk or a lecture. I don't think he ever knew I was a speaker. He never needed to.

I met Karen at a retreat center when a leader asked if I'd speak with her privately. I found her in the counseling room, red-eyed with flecks of wet tissue on her cheek. Forty-two years old, intelligent and attractive, Karen's broken dream was not having married. But a man was showing her interest at the moment. A kind man. Attentive. The problem was this man was her boss, and he was already married.

"There's been no affair," Karen said through her tears, "but it's a train wreck waiting to happen. I'm alone. His wife has depression. We work closely together. He's as vulnerable as I am right now."

With a brother that teased her and a father devoid of affection, Karen discovered early on she was susceptible to men's advances. A renewal of faith in her thirties gave her new boundaries to live by, which had stopped her from getting used. But her longing remained, and this glimpse of a love she couldn't have was a torment.

We talked a bit more, then bowed our heads. And in a prayer that was as raw as it was powerful, Karen confessed her temptation, declared her boss off-limits, handed her longing to God, and left the room feeling lighter.

"I'm a private person," she said as we walked down the corridor. "It's a miracle I opened up about this today—and even more so to a man."

Tanya hadn't needed a writer, or Terry a speaker, and it wasn't a broadcaster Karen sought that day. A grandma tends David's grave, not a paid gardener. Marceau's greatest performance came once he stepped off the stage. Remove the mime's makeup, take away the pay. As I discovered in those three moments, as Coleen's life demonstrates, much good can be done beyond a job title.

"This is my commandment," our gospel reading ended this morning: "Love each other in the same way I have loved you."[11]

Love . . .

The force that set heaven's carousels spinning, made the blazing skies, poured forth the oceans. The breath that rustles each delicate leaf. The hand behind the monarch butterfly's flight. The crux of all matters. The reason for existence. The beat of the heart that brought it all into being. Every fine eyelash, each fluttering wing, every tall tree that springs from each tiny seed whispers of a love that created this world for the sheer joy of sharing it.

. . . each other . . .

The one thing that matters. Our primary work. God's mission shared: *love each other.* The force that makes saints give royal horses to paupers, tend to weeping mothers, shed tears with friends with bad news. The wind in the sail. The current in the wire. The light that makes even the toughest life glisten.

The impulse that turns ice cream shops into communities. Turns cities into homes. Makes friends out of strangers.

. . . the same way I have loved you.

The source. The model. Our pattern to follow. The maker of the heavens kneeling in the dust. The hands that move the stars bathing dirty feet. The ruler of the oceans tending a sick child. Opening closed eyes. Blessing his enemies. The breath that stirs the leaf groaning in agony. A butterfly pinned down. Sacrifice.

The Father prunes in preparation for a new season. And maybe for me that's meant a stripping back to things I've known but not fully grasped.

Like the fact that there's only one real calling, whatever our job or career path—one great river from which all the streams of life flow: *to love God and love others.*

That's it. Nothing more.[12]

So when one stream ends, go back up the river and simply love those standing before you.

CHAPTER 7

THE SPACE IN BETWEEN

I squint at the clock. Red digits tell me it's 4:52 a.m. The guy in the next room is snoring loudly, and his TV has been on all night, playing talk show reruns and ads for online casinos. I roll over and stare at the ceiling. Wallpaper peels; paint is flaking. I should just get up.

The dinginess of these walls reflects the change of scenery we'd experienced yesterday as we approached the hotel. The open fields had turned to scrub and weeds had appeared in the asphalt's edges. Soon we were walking past coal piles and smoke and rusty steel fences, with pylons in the distance like six-armed gods clutching cables in their fists.

We had skirted a large power station and a decommissioned aluminum smelter, DJ limping slightly and my heels so sore I treaded flat-footed. Shuffling along that litter-strewn road, we'd reached a housing estate, rows of identical brick homes lining treeless lanes with only an occasional satellite dish for decoration. The street had been empty apart from a man on a bicycle. As he approached us, a door had flung open and a tracksuit-clad woman charged across her lawn, her finger pointed like a pistol.

"Don't you ever f*****g swear at my bl***y son again!" she'd yelled.

"I never f*****g swore at your bl***y son," he shouted back.

"You f*****g well did—Tommy bl***y-well told me!"

And there the two had continued trading expletives about swearing at children while the woman's three kids watched from her front door.

We'd reached our hotel twenty minutes later, a small establishment in the main street across from a boarded-up pub with a busted-up Nissan parked out front. After repeated knocks on the door, a cheerless caretaker had finally let us in, and a sense of unease had settled on me about the place.

Resigned to starting the day, I hobble into a bathroom of brown-and-orange tiles and run the shower for a good ten minutes. The water doesn't even get warm. Another room is vacant (quite a few in fact), and I later shower down the hall. And after a greasy breakfast on chipped laminate tables, DJ and I pull on our jackets, pull up our hoods, and step out that hotel door into a cold, wet, blustery day.

We walk up the main street past the fast-food restaurants and liquor stores. There are For Rent signs in windows, and the shutters are down on the discount shops. Some early-rising locals are about. They look us up and down. DJ greets a few but none say hello. For the first time on the trip the mood feels frosty.

A side street leads to a beachside road and a row of homes with ocean views. These will be worth a mint one day when jobs return. From the sports field on, the rain begins in earnest, pelting the ground of the cliffs we climb and the broken fence along its eroding edges. The uphill walk makes me wince. My feet hurt already.

"How far did you say we have to go today?" I ask.

"Eighteen miles," DJ says.

I put my pack down and start rummaging for pills.

I can feel a headache coming on.

———

Overcast days aren't so bad. They can evoke memories like an old black-and-white photograph. A walk in the rain, too, can be fun. Senses spark under a downpour. On another day I could enjoy these cliffs more, even in their sodden state. But a sore head and the fog of sleeplessness put a melancholy cast on all I see.

The precipice descends to a beach of stone and boulder. When the sand appears, we step on and trudge our way across the gray grit. No frolicking dogs today, and the birds are staying dry under leaf. Even the weather strikes an unwelcome tone, a northerly wind slapping each raindrop in our faces.

A low tide makes the beach wide, and the distant shore makes the sea seem quiet, so when a low-level rushing grows louder, it's not the ocean we hear.

"How did we miss that?" I say, as we near the source of the roar.

A large stream courses toward the ocean. Broken only by a

few small sandbars, it stretches several meters wide. I pull out the map and find our location. What seemed a mere tributary on paper was in fact the mouth of a river.

"Maybe there's another way around," DJ says.

"Only if we go inland to this bridge," I say, pointing to the map. The detour could add a half hour of walking time. My feet sure do hurt.

DJ skirts the stream, looking for shallow spots. I ponder the gap between sandbars and wonder if I can clear them. As DJ wades into the freezing water I take a leap, come up short, splash ankle deep, then sink farther down as the current flushes sand from under my boots. We both emerge drenched from the shins down.

We drag our sopping feet up the beach to a rock and wring our socks and empty our shoes. I see DJ now has several blisters on each foot.

"How far did you say we have to go again?"

I remember that night I was sitting at Kangaroo Point overlooking Brisbane, I had reminisced about my first flat. It was in a big old house converted to single rooms, mine being the smallest. The space was just large enough for a bed and a small desk, and the kitchen was so tight you could reach sink, fridge, and stove without getting up from the table. After my first night there, I bought a pack of roach bombs. But the rent was cheap.

A cast of characters lived around me. Sal the landlord was a kindly Italian who never remembered my name, writing rent receipts to "Sheldon Voyeur" one week and "Stefan Wyzley" the next. White-haired Joe lived in the front room and still wore his wedding ring after losing his wife decades ago. Across the hall was Matt, a wild-eyed thirtysomething Elijah figure who smoked weed and talked about aliens a lot. And next door was Keith, a barrel-chested, book-loving, ex-army man as gentle as a Labrador, with whom I'd often talk about life and sometimes pray.

Some nights I'd hear a radio on. It always seemed to emanate from a room at the back of the house with its own stairs, but I'd never seen anyone come or go. Then one morning I woke to a faint cry for help. Peering outside, I found a frail old man in his underwear collapsed at the bottom of the stairs.

"Oh thank God!" he said on seeing me. "I fell from the bl***y top step."

I put an arm under his shoulder and tried easing him up, but he swore in pain. "You may have broken something," I said. "I'll call an ambulance."

"I'll be all right," he said firmly. "Just get me back to my room."

At that moment the downstairs toilet flushed, and out walked a bleary-eyed Matt. "What's up with Victor?" he said. At first grateful for his timely appearance, I soon did a double take. Matt had nothing on but a T-shirt.

Half-naked Matt helped me wrestle Victor up the stairs while the old man shouted obscenities. On reaching the top, I tried backing in through the door, but my way was blocked. I soon saw why: rubbish. Mountains of it, knee-high throughout Victor's room. There were newspapers, bottles, soup cans, pizza boxes, plastic bags full of heaven-knew-what, and a bin brimming with festering food scraps. The smell of urine and rot was so strong I nearly retched. It would burn in my nostrils for days.

A sagging mattress sat in the corner, its sheets stained with sweat. We climbed over the rubbish and laid Victor down. Dirty dinner plates had been pushed under the bed and drinking glasses sat caked with stale milk. Squalid brown smears streaked across the wall and in the corner sat the demons behind it all— empty wine flagons.

Victor had broken some ribs, but when the ambulance arrived he refused the help. Joe told me Victor's only known kin was an estranged wife living much the same way. When Victor was later rushed to hospital, Sal cleared out his room. I visited his ward and found him unconscious. Then I moved away. Whatever became of him?

I took away many things from that first flat experience, one proving unexpectedly helpful now. With the cleaning of amenities left to us motley tenants, it wasn't surprising I caught an infection from the communal shower that left the skin of my feet dry and tough. All these years later, that coarse skin is the reason only DJ has the blisters.

In that flat I learned to live simply, too, cooking one-pot meals on my little stove, spreading textbooks across my bed as a makeshift desk, enduring humid summers in that closet of a room that rained dust when you bumped its walls. But perhaps what I really took from that time was an awareness of life's hard edges. When Joe couldn't bear to talk about his wife, or Matt became erratic after getting high, or Victor's frail frame returned to mind, any naïve notions I had about the world were tempered. The textbooks on my bed spoke of heaven, but heaven hadn't arrived next door.

One day I was leaving my flat just as kindly Keith came walking up the hall. I noticed him swaying a little, his steps cautious, his army-built arms bumping the walls. When he saw me, he stopped and hid his face. Then he burst into tears.

"Please don't think less of me!" he pleaded.

After years off the bottle, Keith had taken a tumble, medicating wounds deeper than I could see with an afternoon's sitting at a bar.

"Please don't think less of me," he whispered again, fumbling the key to his door.

Oh, Keith, how could I?

Drips hang from the edge of my cap. Trousers cling wet to my legs. My padded boots slurped so much sea I squelch and suck with each step. The rain has eased, but that northerly still blows. I put my hands in my pockets, starting to shiver.

From beach to path and path to road we push ourselves through the morning, passing quarries and stoneworks, truck bays and warehouses, a concrete plant and the abandoned site of a once-mighty power station. In the distance there's a port with wharves and tankers. It has piles of coal and silos with conveyor belts.

Britain birthed the Industrial Revolution, shaping the world through textile mills and steel smelters that gave us parts for cars, fabric for clothes, bricks to build homes, and power for our sockets. From books to biscuits to flushable toilets, much of what makes life enjoyable now comes from a factory.

But try as I might, such merits can't lift the gloom I feel at our industrial surroundings. Gone are the valleys with their winding rivers and the patchwork meadows stitched with hedgerows. Gone are the miles of mirrored clouds and the secret caves in the woods. No majestic ruins glint on the horizon, just cables, cranes, and silos. There are no flower boxes or dry-stone walls, just weeds and rusty fences.

Something else is missing, too—our muse, Cuthbert. We've left the hills where we know he wandered. His island retreats are far behind us. As best we know, Cuthbert's monks carried his coffin farther west of here as they made their way to Durham. Any lines once drawn to Aidan and Oswald have equally faded too.

If Cuthbert did walk here, we have no record of it happening. And if there's splendor to be found in this concrete and steel, I haven't the eyes to see it.

Give me a new cave. Show me another castle.

I'm not enjoying this walk anymore.

———

The port is large, and its harbor splits into two wide rivers that fork apart, requiring a three-mile turn inland and the crossing of two bridges to navigate around them. We follow the old power station road toward a busy highway and the first bridge. The headache pills haven't worked. My head is thumping.

"We haven't talked about your trip yet," DJ says. "How was it?"

If I were at home right now I'd be sitting in a quiet room with the blinds drawn, waiting for my headache to pass. Without that option, conversation may be the next best remedy, providing something else to focus on.

I search the sky and the grass and the road for words to answer DJ's question, as it's something I'm still processing. "It was *surprising*," I say.

A few weeks ago I'd had the opportunity to share the message of my book through a short speaking tour. At each event I told Merryn's and my story with all its sadness, anger, and hidden humor, and the steps we'd taken to start afresh. I had soon discovered that something special happens when you share your life candidly: people entrust you with their own secrets.

This was evident from the first talk I gave. "We were missionaries in Africa," a woman confided afterward. "Then our daughter got depressed. That led to drug use, then to self-harm. Then she took her life. Missionaries had to look 'successful' back then, and losing a child to suicide wasn't a mark of spiritual success, so I couldn't tell anyone what happened. Even now, few people know."

A professional man in his fifties had approached me next. "We adopted two children from the Philippines," he said, "one of whom we discovered has autism. He gets violent and reduces my wife to tears by screaming at her. Our marriage is under pressure because we disagree on how to deal with him." The man looked over his shoulder and lowered his voice. "We've served God all our lives. What did we do to deserve a child who kicks in our walls?"

"I used to be an evangelist," said another man. "Then my four-month-old son died." He pointed to his head: "I say I trust God." Then he pointed to his heart: "But I don't really *trust* God. But I can't tell many people that."

"Person after person pulled me aside," I tell DJ, "telling of lost marriages, lost careers, shaken faith, broken dreams. Somehow I'd entered an inner circle where all the secrets are told. It was like being initiated into a new tribe."

The tribe metaphor fits, the more I reflect on it. In many

primitive cultures, membership to a tribe is granted only after an initiate has endured some painful trials. They're taken into the wilderness, told the tribe's stories, put through difficulty, then scarred with the tribe's markings. There's no entrance without wounds, no inclusion without scars. Merryn and I had spent ten years in the wilderness of infertility, and our wounds from that time had become our initiation marks. In writing the book and sharing our story, I had proverbially bared those scars and been invited in.

"And then I got to see God work."

Traffic noise builds as we approach the highway. A semi-trailer rumbles past us, spraying gritty mist kicked up by its tires from the wet road.

"What happened?" DJ asks, flicking water from the rim of his hood.

I push my thumbs under my pack straps to ease the load on my hips, and ponder which story to share. I think first of a lady who attended a conference session.

"She'd experienced not one, not two, but *eight* miscarriages," I say, "followed by the heartache of an adoption falling through. She told me she'd been stuck in this grief for years, defined by her losses, but had been able to hand her broken dream over to God that night and could now move on with her life."

"Wow. That's pretty special."

"Another woman came to the front of the auditorium in tears. She was on medication for a blood disease and had just been told she needed a heart transplant. The cruel twist was the drugs she took for the blood disease would almost certainly make her body reject a new heart. She's only in her forties."

DJ expels a breath of sympathy.

"She asked me to pray for her. I assumed she wanted prayer for healing or maybe guidance, but I was wrong. She looked at me through her tears and said, 'I've turned away from God because of all this. Today I want to turn back to him.'"

Most of the stories had been less dramatic. Some had left my talks comforted to know they weren't alone in their plight. Others simply left hopeful for a brighter day. But at times the sense of God's working had felt uncanny.

"A guy came up after I spoke at a church one night," I add. "He said, 'I haven't been to church in twenty-six years, but all week I had this strange feeling I should get to a service. I've been through a divorce, I just lost my business—what you shared tonight was exactly what I needed to hear. It's almost like I was meant to be here.' I said I believed he *was* meant to be there and got him connected with the church.

"Immediately after him a couple walked up. 'I haven't been to church in years,' the guy said. 'And I've never been to church,' said the girl. 'But all week we had this strange feeling we should get to a service. And what you shared tonight was exactly what we needed to hear. It's almost like we were meant to be here.'"

DJ laughs.

"Like I said—*surprising*."

The conversation is, indeed, good distraction, making me less conscious of my headache and my smarting feet, which feel as if someone has taken a hammer to them. We come closer to the river, the bridge in view, and another story comes to mind.

"It's unfair how much some have to cope with, though," I say. "Like this woman I met, Susan. She'd broken her leg and was immobile for weeks after complications with the surgery. She needed help washing, dressing, and getting to work. A couple of months into her recovery, Susan's husband left her for another woman."

"Charming," DJ says.

"It got worse. Susan's mother passed away soon after that. Then she was laid off. Within weeks Susan had lost her health, husband, mother, and job. Her first question to me was *why*—why was all this happening to her?

"But Susan came up to me again after I'd spoken, and something about her seemed different. She said, 'I came thinking my question was *why*, but I realize now my real question is *who*—who am I? When your husband leaves and your boss fires you, you start feeling unwanted. But I wrote something down while you were speaking tonight, words I've never written before.' She opened her notebook and began to cry. She'd written *I am a child of God* across the page."

Our path starts to climb as the road rises to meet the highway. We push past some wet overhanging scrub that showers us with drips.

A missionary once told me a fascinating story. He was working in Estonia and saw many deaf Estonians become Christians. Having come to believe in a miracle-working God, these deaf Christians had started praying fervently for their healing. And God did wonders—miraculously restoring the hearing of two of them. But with the miracle came an unexpected consequence.

"Immediately afterward," the missionary told me, "the two who were healed found themselves outside the deaf community. That's when the others realized their deafness was a gift that enabled them to reach people no one else could."

No entrance without wounds, no inclusion without scars.

But once you're inside the tribe, you have something to offer.

We stop on the bridge as cars rush by, their tires swishing water across the lanes. I rest my arms on the wet steel railing, too weary to care that it soaks my sleeves. The river below flows dark and oily. There are old tires and trolleys on its banks.

Hands freezing. Trousers soaked. Rain tapping on the hoods of our raincoats. Five days ago we had faced this same kind of weather with arms swinging and stars in our eyes. Today we stumble along on our pilgrim-song, our feet off beat and our tune discordant. We have miles to go but have already stopped four times.

"We should've planned in a rest day," I say, lifting a heel to soothe it.

"We could never have done that and arrived on time," DJ replies.

Neither of us had been able to start the pilgrimage earlier, leaving us just eight days to reach Durham before the Lindisfarne Gospels left town. We're booked in to see them Monday morning, the last week of the exhibition, so we must reach Durham by Sunday. That's three and a half days left to walk a further fifty miles.

"If we really need a break we have only one option," he adds.

We'll need to take a shortcut.

Some years ago Merryn and I took a holiday to Japan. We visited Osaka's grand castle, saw Kyoto's Golden Pavilion, watched cosplay kids wander Tokyo's neon streets, and ate cross-legged on tatami mats in a traditional ryokan inn. Geisha in colorful kimonos, monkeys in hot springs. It was a memorable vacation.

The highlight for me had been Nagano, where we'd tried our hand at skiing. Not that it had started well. Underestimating the time required to wade through the snow and rent our gear, we'd missed the beginner's class, taken the chairlift to the wrong field, and caused such gasps from onlookers by our twisting and crashing that we'd unstrapped our skis mid-slope and trodden forlornly home.

The wonder had begun on day two. Accompanied by instructors, we'd taken the lift to the top of the mountain for views of speechless splendor: snowcapped peaks in every direction, velvet slopes flowing like cream, skiers in the hundreds sprinkled like confetti, chairlifts rising into mist. On reaching the top we slid onto the gentle descent of the beginners' slope and learned to balance and turn more confidently.

By midafternoon we were ready for a rest, but when a Japanese skier said he'd take me farther afield, I found the energy to accept the offer.

"I take you to Diamond Mountain," he said in his broken English.

"Are the slopes very steep?" I asked. "I'm new to this."

"Very easy slope, no crash," he assured me.

His name was Toyo, and for the next two hours he led me from crest to crest in this fairy-tale land via a series of slopes and chairlifts. Toyo would zoom down each hill, then wait while I tumbled after him. His definition of "easy" clearly wasn't mine.

"What do you do for work?" I asked as we took a cable car ride.

"I don't work." He smiled. "I do this."

"You ski every day?" I clarified.

"Except Saturdays," he said. "Too many people then."

Toyo told me he was originally an architect. Having built a large and successful architectural firm, he had then sold it and retired at the age of forty-three. Now he skied all winter and played golf in the summer, living off the interest from the sale.

"You don't do anything else?" I asked, fishing for something that might somehow contribute to humanity. He said he did do other things: "I watch movies, too, and I soak in my hot tub."

Clear sky, powder-soft snow, frosted trees sparkling like crystal. Icicles hung from our airborne chairs. I kept expecting Narnia's Mr. Tumnus to appear. But as I tumbled through this magical afternoon, Toyo's leisure-filled days troubled me. A life of skiing, movies, and hot tubs felt a little vacuous, especially in a world of need. Toyo didn't seem to have many friends, and when I asked about a family he just said "pretty wife." It sounded more like a hope than a reality.

We returned to base, I thanked Toyo for his time, and with a push on his poles he slid off to another slope. Maybe I read him wrong. Maybe I was overanalyzing things. But as I headed home I wondered to myself:

What part of your life, Toyo, are you avoiding?

It's another mile along the highway before we reach the second river, its banks equally greasy. Cables hang by the dozen above us, slinking back to the defunct power station. We cross the canal and take an exit ramp left onto a busy suburban road.

Before long we've stopped again to ease our feet and adjust our loads.

"Would it be a cop-out to cut today's walk short?" I say.

"Or would we be giving our bodies the rest they need?" DJ wonders.

We shuffle off again, pondering together whether catching a lift to the next town would be an act of weakness or wisdom.

The concept of pilgrimage most of us hold today harks back to the Middle Ages. The pilgrim's journey was understood as being an intentional walk to a holy place to receive some kind of blessing. The place may have been the shrine of a saint or a sacred well; the blessing could have been forgiveness or healing. But what mattered most was reaching the destination—that's where the blessing was received.

The Celtic idea of pilgrimage was different. For them, a destination was rarely in mind. They set out directionless into the wild or let their coracles drift wherever the currents took them. Pilgrimage for the Celt was an act of voluntary exile, leaving the comfort and security of home to be in complete abandonment to God. Any benefit to them wasn't waiting at the end—it was found along the journey.[1]

What the Celtic and medieval conceptions did share was a belief that pilgrimage should be demanding. In the Dark Ages this was taken to ludicrous lengths as troubled souls walked on their knees or put stones in their shoes to win God's favor. While Celtic pilgrimage lacked this fault, it was still an intense enterprise. Celtic spirituality was rigorously physical and included praying for hours in a cruciform shape or reciting psalms in the freezing sea, fasting for days or going without sleep to bring the body into godly submission. The Christian was a nomad en route to heaven, and a pilgrimage reminded him or her of this.[2] It was an exacting tool that weaned the Christian's soul from worldly allures to make it content in God alone.

So I can only imagine how the seventh-century pilgrim would roll his eyes at our warm motels and headache pills. While they foraged for food and slept in the rain, I complain about cold showers and search for a shortcut home.

We come to a bus stop. DJ checks the timetable, and I tell myself even the sturdiest Celt would rest after five days' walking.

But checking that board still feels like a cop-out.

———

There won't be a bus for another half hour, so we trundle on down the road. A car dealership on our left. A school to our right. A Chinese restaurant ahead. We've hit suburbia. Soon the yellow arches of a fast-food chain appear above the telephone wires. It's been a while since I saw that ubiquitous symbol.

We approach a large parking lot with shops on three sides— furniture, home wares, affordable bathroom tiles—all big-box stores made of concrete and steel offering hassle-free loans on easy-to-read signs. A car wash comes next, then a bus depot. An office block, then a drive-through chicken shop.

No misty hills, no Celtic magic.

It all feels so soulless.

What hypocrisy—turning up my nose at the very things I use. I've shopped at those "soulless" stores before, wandered those dealerships, eaten beneath those yellow arches. Hidden within my sentiment is the unrealistic belief that convenience can exist without unsightly structures. I want buses but not depots, biscuits but not factories, toilets without sewage plants, lights without power lines. I want none of life's ugliness and all of its beauty. That simply cannot be.

The rain has eased but the temperature has plummeted. I breathe into my hands, rub them together, but they stay as blue and frozen as my cheeks. My raincoat is so soaked it's damp inside. My shoulders quiver from the chill.

In his book *The Second Journey*, Gerald O'Collins divides life into three stages. The first is from childhood to maturity; the third, from old age to death. In between is a middle course that can be difficult and lonely—where the power of youth fades, failure now has consequences, and once-settled identities are challenged or lost. This is a tumultuous stage of disappointment and confusion, but can lead to new wisdom and purpose when navigated well.[3]

Along the hard terrain of this second stage are many tempting detours. Promising to be shortcuts, they instead lead to dead ends, bringing our journeys to a halt. One winds off into darkened fields of addiction—afternoons in bars to dull the memories, puffs of weed to escape, another swig of the bottle while the rubbish piles up and flagons fill the room. Another detour leads to pleasurable distractions—illicit affairs or shopping sprees; endless movies, hot tubs, and days on powdery slopes—safe places in our imaginations where ugly reality can be avoided. It's all lies.

Because there's an in-between time in every journey, in every pilgrimage, in every life when the excitement of our starting dwindles away and our ebullient march ebbs to a shuffle, when the beauty disappears and the magic lifts and the stars fall from our eyes. And in this in-between time, as we ache and shiver and wonder why we keep going because the meaning is missing, we have choices to make.

We can grab the bottle, hit the slopes, take whatever diversion promises an escape, or retreat into a world of memories past, yearning for their misty hills and glowing horizons— and when the fingers snap and we wake from our nostalgia, or we find ourselves trapped in some squalid place, we discover we're no further along in our journey. Avoidance has kept us in stage two.

Or we can choose to face reality as it is—its weeds, rust, and flaking paint included; its failures, miscarriages, and identity crises; reality in all its ordinariness. And by facing that reality for as long as it takes—submitting to its questions, learning its lessons, taking it on, staring it down, punctuating it with rest and what laughter we can muster—we may stumble on to find new wisdom and purpose, maybe also a tribe that needs us, and be surprised by the gifts we now have to offer.

※

After the drive-through comes a supermarket. Then a retirement home, then a tire store. And as we follow the suburban road around the corner, we find we need to stop once more. A knee-high wall runs along the footpath. We drop our bags and sit down.

I wiggle my toes inside my socks. They rub numb against the wet wool. I pull out my phone to check the time. My fingers won't flex for the cold. It's midday, and we have another nine miles to go. Time to make a decision. My teeth are chattering, my head still hurts. I pull my arms tight to my sides to keep warm.

I'm still averse to taking a shortcut. Wouldn't it be an act of avoidance in itself? Maybe not. If anything, an afternoon's rest will help us face tomorrow's difficulty, not escape it, while pressing on could do damage that jeopardizes our reaching the end.

"Do you think it's a sign?" DJ says, smiling. He points to an off-duty taxi parked in the street with a phone number emblazoned on its door.

I breathe on my fingers then return to my phone.

And dial the number.

CHAPTER 8

LOSING AND BIRTHING

You need the toilet.
    I don't care.
But you're busting.
    Leave me alone.

I lie halfway off the bed like some awkwardly reclining puppy—my heels on the floor to keep my boots off the linen, my back on the mattress, my arms spread in opposite directions. Having cast off my jacket when I first walked in I'd then slumped while untying my laces. That was twenty minutes ago.

Nine miles in a taxi had taken just a few minutes. Now the afternoon is for rest. Cop-out or not, I clearly need it. I push myself up and start pulling off my boots, shaking each foot free to a thousand hallelujahs, and consider walking to the shared amenities down the corridor.

I fall back on the bed instead.

I can wait a bit longer.

No you can't.

Go away.

But as the pain gets worse, I finally obey my body, scuffing flat-footed down the carpeted hall, my soles raw, my clammy socks leaving steamy prints on the bathroom linoleum, then return to plant my face on the pillow.

I want it back—that feeling I had on Lindisfarne, when one foot followed the other along the bare north shore while waves slid across the sand and a voice whispered, **Attend, attend**. That feeling as I walked through the swaying marram grass, listening to the song of the seals carried on the wind. That feeling of a soul at peace and a mind at rest that I'm not feeling anymore.

All I feel right now is tired. Not the nice kind of tired you feel after a morning's work in the yard but the depleting, jittery exhaustion that leaves you restless. We have only three days left to get to Durham, which seems like both an eternity and not nearly enough time. I hate feeling rushed, yet feel inadequate for taking this time off too.

My body is lead; my head sinks into the pillow. As I suck in breath I realize this is not an unfamiliar predicament for me. I've felt this all before.

———

Before moving into that shoebox of a flat, I spent my first two years of college living on campus. There I'd boarded with another array of characters—a Harley-riding psychiatric nurse with a handlebar moustache, a Led Zeppelin–loving farmer decked in cowboy boots, and a fuzzy-haired roommate who snored and rarely washed his clothes. Those two years were reeking and sleepless.

The college was led by a principal for whom sleeplessness was never more than a small irritant. This man not only directed the college and lectured in its classes but also led a church, sat on numerous boards, took overseas speaking gigs, even helped run a chain of retail stores. I didn't think at the time to include that he was also a husband and father. He was a gifted, disciplined achiever.

For reasons only Freud might fathom, my twentysomething self saw in this man a benchmark of Christian success. *Look at all he's doing,* I thought. *Surely, then, you can add some radio work, a counseling course, and a part-time job to your study load.*

Well, no, I couldn't. And at midnight one evening I arrived at my parents' door asking for my old bed back, suffering from acute insomnia and exhaustion.

Busyness is a bully at the best of times. Strong and greedy, it wants the playground for itself and so forces all else to flee. It chases peace away first, then patience, then kindness, before stomping out love and joy and self-control. Busyness whistles and hollers and kicks up the dust. It clouds things up and drowns things out.

But this bully gets worse when it hangs around comparison. Then it becomes a tyrant. As comparison points out someone afar—showing us all they're doing and the success they're achieving—busyness pounces on our backs and rides us hard. *You're not good enough!* it taunts. *Do more. Try harder. Then you might be like them.*

If only I could say such voices were stilled as I worked through that early burnout. But when college ended and I became a youth worker—and the kid had his accident and the girl went through the courts and the guy locked himself in the room and I started falling apart—*You're not good enough!* was what I heard.

And after that, when radio doors opened and I listened to other stations while driving home from work, hearing announcers who were smarter and funnier than I with better shows and deeper voices, *You're not professional enough!* rang loud. Soon I was seeing a speech therapist to fix a busted voice I'd forced too low.

Then later again, walking through the wilderness with Merryn, searching for a child that wouldn't be found, that same voice had whispered. Because if I'd had enough faith surely the ground would've trembled, the mountain been uprooted, our childlessness hurled into the sea. But others got the miracle while Merryn and I waited, and *You're not spiritual enough!* became my refrain.

I roll onto my side and stare at the parted brown curtains, readjusting my arm when it starts to ache from being pressed into the mattress.

You don't see Cuthbert comparing himself to others. But then, you don't see him having many faults at all. Maybe this is part of our problem. Cuthbert's biographers present him as the archetypal saint: so humble he washes the feet of his visitors, so wise he enlightens everyone he counsels, so powerful he quells a raging fire with a word, so holy he turns water into wine just by tasting it.[1] Otters dry his feet with their breath after he prays all night in the sea.[2] People get healed touching his clothes, wearing his shoes, or drinking the water used to wash his dead body.[3] The nearest we come to seeing a weakness in Cuthbert is his fear of falling to the love of riches.[4] But with godly restraint and a diet of raw onions, it's a temptation he deftly avoids.

Through exaggerated biographies and airbrushed news feeds, our heroes often come to us without stain or crease— glorious, victorious, and flaw-free. Or else we see them on a stage with their talents on show but their support crew neatly concealed. Seeing only their perfections or ignoring their helpers, we're given a false standard to follow.

Busyness, writes David Whyte, is a sure sign that we are living someone else's life and doing someone else's work.[5] My principal was an achiever but also thirty years my senior, with different capacities than I. And maybe others could do this journey without needing this break. Should yesteryear's pilgrim roll his eyes, so be it. If Cuthbert had a halo, he also had shadows, and a calling different than mine.

I get up from the bed and shut the curtains, sucking my teeth with each tender step, then return and lie down on my back.

Time to accept my limits, however confining they are. To stop chasing others' lives and embrace my own. To silence the voices, quit the comparisons.

To close these eyes and rest awhile.

———

Another piece of toast. A second cup of coffee. Clothes packed slowly. A soft start to the day. By the time we step outside the sun has risen, stark autumn light bleaching the stately homes of Whitley Bay. A promenade rides high along the winding coastline with parks and swings and sea-facing benches. Ramps lead down to small coves and beaches, and boathouses nestle in the cliffs.

What a difference one night can make. Waves whisper softly, flowers bloom on roundabouts, the beauty I missed yesterday having returned. The effect on me is noticeable—I feel more buoyant, more joyful. I can even see a castle ahead.

We start walking along the promenade and within minutes reach a south-heading bus taking passengers. A night on the heater hasn't dried my boots, my feet still hurt, my back and hips ache. But we don't get on. Yesterday's respite has bought us some miles.

We take that promenade all the way to Tynemouth, enjoying its elevation, looking down on the rolling sea, gently winding higher as we go. And as the path curves left to climb a headland, we gain an aerial view of a small bay. The tide freshly out, the sand still wet, the beach shimmers like cellophane with flashes of silver and teal and scratches of tan from sandbars breaking through the reflected sky.

Groups of students are using sticks and their hands to etch designs on the shore, while high above them, on the tip of the promontory, stand the ruins of the castle. And not just a castle, we find, but an eleventh-century priory. High and jagged, its cathedral-like walls rest on even deeper history, the first monastery on the site dating to Cuthbert's time. As Lindisfarne bustled with monks about their work, another band of brothers was doing the same here.

I'm reminded of a small priory not far from our home in Oxford that's run by the Carmelites. No cathedral-style walls or stone arches there, just a small chapel, a house for the brothers, and simple rooms you can hire for prayer. On occasions when busyness has whistled and hollered, I've hiked up the hill to book in for a day.

My last visit was quite recent, on return from my speaking trip. A morning of prayerful solitude had helped settle the dust but also revealed that I should talk to someone. After sharing this with one of the staff, an Irish friar appeared at my door wearing a brown habit, a woolen skullcap, and a kind, approachable expression.

"What should I call you?" I'd asked as we walked to a meeting room, my ignorance of monastic etiquette showing. "Is it Father, Brother, or—"

"Call me Liam," he said, offering me a seat. "Shall we start with a prayer?"

While keen to pray, I hoped Liam wouldn't get too Catholic on me. Things could get awkward for this Protestant if he beseeched a saint or Mother Mary.

"Holy Trinity," he began, "Father, Son, and Holy Spirit . . ."
Pretty good so far.
". . . guide our hearts and minds now . . ."
Not bad, indeed.
". . . be in our meditation and our conversation . . ."
I like this guy.
". . . for Christ's sake and your glory."
"Amen!" I said.
"And Holy Mother, pray for us now . . ."

I laughed inside and veiled my scruples in a few extra moments of silent prayer. When I opened my eyes, I found Liam waiting patiently.

"Maybe it's because I'm a firstborn," I said, "or because I was an only child for the first twelve years of my life, but my natural tendency is to try to work things out on my own. I guess I'm here to counteract that."

"Very good," Liam said.

I then gave him a summary of Merryn's and my recent years—the dream career and wilderness journey, the IVF rounds and adoption lists, the Christmas Eve phone call and move overseas, the unexpected books, the plastic bags floating in the breeze.

"I guess I'm wondering what my new calling is," I said.

"You're not broadcasting here?" he asked.

"No. I'm not even sure I'm supposed to."

"And how is Merryn doing?"

Having expected the career chat to go a bit further, the question took me by surprise. But it was welcome enough.

"When having children started looking doubtful," I replied, "Merryn began exploring her career options more seriously. She reviewed what she'd been good at in the past, right back to her school years. The result was her choosing a profession many have dreamed of doing but been too afraid to try."

"What was it?" Liam asked.

"Statistics." And we laughed.

While I still had nightmares about sitting through high school math tests, Merryn had followed her aptitude for numbers into the world of medicine and on to projects tackling typhoid, malaria, and other diseases, finding a vocation that was both personally fulfilling and beneficial to others.

"Coming here has been the best move for her," I added. "Oxford University is the leading institution in her field."

"Very good," said Liam, looking pleased.

Merryn had found her place in another sense too. As she'd

searched for a new identity once motherhood was off the table, a passage of Scripture had spoken to her. In the famous Proverbs 31 portrait, the praiseworthy woman isn't only a nurturer of children. She buys and sells property, she invests in industry, and she runs her own business in the clothing trade.[6] She is wise, hardworking, and profitable in these ventures, and helps her husband play a guiding role in the community.[7]

As the numbers girl who sorted our taxes, who found us our homes and negotiated their financing, and whose wage was currently our main source of income given my vocation was up in the air, this passage had validated Merryn for who she already was—a woman with a career that enabled her husband to guide others through his writing and speaking.

"Merryn knows where she fits in the world," I said. "She has a stronger sense of calling than me right now."

"And your marriage," Liam asked next. "How is that going?"

"I thank God for our marriage," I said, still wondering when we'd get back to my first question. "Merryn and I know why infertility can break a couple now: the constant raised and dashed hopes, the moral dilemmas over treatments, the big decisions you have to make when you're not always of one mind. We had a decade of that. We argued, we compromised. But we emerged through it stronger and closer."

"I'm so glad to hear that," Liam said in his gentle Irish accent, wearing a smile as proud as a grandfather's. "Covenant is the core of the gospel—God's covenant with us, our covenants with each other—and marriage is one of the most powerful signs of this to the world. You and Merryn have given yourselves to each other body and soul, in a binding commitment of love and trust, whatever life brings. And you've gone through this trial without that commitment breaking. Oh, the world needs to see that kind of commitment. It gets so few examples of it."

Attend, Sheridan.

"As a fifty-six-year-old celibate under the vow," he continued, "I, of course, know little of what you've been through. But maybe I've glimpsed it. My brother asked me to baptize my nephew recently. And as I held that baby over the baptismal font, it hit me—I'll never have this. I'll never have my own child."

Liam's eyes were full of emotion, yet devoid of self-pity.

"But when we look at Christ, Sheridan, we see all our suffering and more. He never got to enjoy marriage. He never had children. He gave up a thriving ministry, too, when they came to arrest him. When you gave up your radio show for Merryn, you echoed that. You died to self. You may not realize the witness you're having already, beyond what you say or do, simply by being who you are."

Attend.

Liam and I spoke into the early evening. Only toward the end did we sail close to what I'd first wished to discuss.

"How is the book doing?" he asked.

I told him about singles finding peace and couples finding hope, about people being mysteriously drawn to church and broken mothers finding God again.

"It's all a surprise to Merryn and me," I said. "All we've done is told our story."

"Wow," Liam said slowly. "Look what's happening."

I waited, listening.

"The lack of a birth in your life is birthing life in others."

DJ and I walk down from the priory, looking back on that small bay from the other side. With grid lines scratched down, the students gather around their plans before kneeling to score and render with their fingers. One group etches an E, another works on a G, but it will be hours before their letters make meaning. We head down over the grassy promontory, and reach the wide mouth of the River Tyne.

The sun is still out and a gusty breeze cools our sweaty arms. The Tyne here is a wide, watery highway for cruise ships and tankers; a trawler motors past us, and a horn blows in the distance. We walk west along its banks, looking for a ferry terminal, but if we were to follow the river's winding miles farther along we'd find it narrow with each bend, getting smaller and smaller, thinning down to a pencil line.

Smaller and smaller: the phrase speaks something of God. For the one who made stars spring from thoughts and cedars spring from seeds has made his delight in small things clear from the start—birthing a nation from an old, infertile couple, confronting a Pharaoh with a stammering shepherd, routing mighty armies with tiny tribes, and felling a towering giant with a child's stone. If that wasn't enough, he leapt into this tiny world himself—slipping through the planets, past Jupiter and Mars, getting smaller and smaller every inch he fell to become a microscopic dot on an ultrasound. And as he grew and walked our streets it was the small he again drew near to—the weak not the strong, the broke not the wealthy, the hidden and forgotten not the powerful and pretty. The great one of the universe is clearly fond of small, insignificant things.

I have pondered all this before, spoken on it, marveled at it, but now, as seagulls squawk and wind tickles my arms and the waves of the trawler's wake slap against the embankment, I see something in it I've missed.

It's the small who receive God's finest gifts—the poor get his kingdom, the sad get his comfort, the last come first, the humble inherit the earth.[8] The worst of offenders get the greatest grace.[9] In each case the blessing comes proportional to the lack. Then notice how these little ones become God's star players—children become teachers, teens become prophets, peasants become the salt of the earth and the light of the world.[10] Weak people become conduits of divine life and strength. Their impact comes proportional to their lowliness.

Paul the apostle stumbled onto this dynamic. Chased, flogged, imprisoned, abandoned—from the moment he fell from his horse into a life of service, hardship was never far away. Yet with each loss of freedom, safety, or status, he found a gap open up through which God's power could flow. He came to see weakness as integral to his mission.[11] When trouble came to Paul, life flowed to others.[12]

So what if each crack in our hearts and every hole in our lives—from the loss of our health or status or power to our lack of a spouse or a child or a career—was the gap through which divine grace waited to flow? What if our humbled status made us ready for the using, our sufferings poised to bring little resurrections?

What if our empty spaces became channels for God's power, our lack birthing new life in others?

The Tyne is awash in the murmurs of industry. Shipbuilders are at work on the other side of the river; cranes load coal onto tankers up ahead; there are fish markets, an export dock, a large scrap-metal yard. And a memory surfaces as we walk, perhaps triggered by the scrap, of a film I saw about a community in Paraguay.

Desperately poor, the villagers in that community had formed an orchestra by crafting instruments from recycled garbage. Violins were made from oil cans with bent forks as tailpieces. Saxophones were made from drainpipes with bottle tops for keys. Cellos came from tin drums with gnocchi rollers for tuning pegs. Hearing the villagers play Mozart on those contraptions was a beautiful thing.[13]

Violins from slums, concertos from rubbish dumps. *It's the kind of thing God does*, I think. And the more one ponders it, the more one can see such a dynamic at work, shaping the world for good.

You can see it in the sweaty bodies that once labored in America's south, picking and scrubbing for their owners' benefit. When simple songs started forming on their lips—about chariots swinging low, about crossing the River Jordan, songs to stoke hope for their own liberation—they never knew what was to come. Those tunes would spread, carrying hope with them, and the new genre of gospel music would be born.

You can see it in Bill and Bob, both battling the bottle, meeting one day to discuss their recovery. Turning their lives over to God, they codify twelve steps to move forward. The steps spread, sobriety follows, and Alcoholics Anonymous is born.

You can see it at work in the story of Joni, left quadriplegic from a diving accident. She visits faith healers for a cure, praying desperately to walk again. The miracle never comes, but what happens instead? One of the most remarkable organizations to serve the disabled is formed.[14]

Or what about St. Patrick, in the fourth century, returning to the land that enslaved him and giving birth to the Irish church? Or the illiterate slave woman Sojourner Truth becoming a fearless preacher for abolition? Or torture survivor Sheila Cassidy becoming a champion of human rights? Or John Bunyan writing *Pilgrim's Progress* from jail, giving us one of the best books of all time?

Yes, the books—so many of the best born also from weakness. Like Dietrich Bonhoeffer's *The Cost of Discipleship*, written under the breath of the Nazis, and Aleksandr Solzhenitsyn's *The Gulag Archipelago*, penned inside Russia's labor camps, and Corrie ten Boom's *The Hiding Place*, rising from the smoke of the gas chambers, and Simone Weil's *Waiting on God*, born from her migraines. Martin Luther King's *Letter from a Birmingham Jail* arose from injustice. C. S. Lewis's *A Grief Observed* emerged from loss. And had a sickly kitchen hand named Brother Lawrence not written from his trials, we wouldn't have *The Practice of the Presence of God*.

And I have seen this life-from-lack dynamic, too, in many I've met. Like the man whose wife was murdered by their son who now helps others learn to forgive, and the guy who lost a leg in a motorcycle crash who now runs camps to help teen amputees, and the woman who told me having a stillborn son led to her career helping parents of disabled children. Then there was the lady I met at a retreat center once whose prayers for the hurting carried such power. No one knew that she'd twice tried to take her own life—her secret wounds now a channel of blessing.

DJ and I reach a waterfront strip of restaurants and cafés, a pleasant break in the industrial surrounds. Families meander, children skip about, a daughter and mother walk arm in arm, and another turn is taken in my wandering thoughts.

"My daughter and I would like to ask a question," I hear in my memory.

The woman I recall had approached me on my speaking trip. Her adult daughter had stood beside her but was too distraught to talk, so she had gone ahead.

"Last year my daughter's husband was arrested for indecent dealings with children," she said, "including their own fourteen-year-old daughter. Since then Kate has lost her husband *and* her daughter—who thinks she must've been complicit—as well as most of her friends. No one wants to be associated with something like this."

I grimaced at the injustice of it.

"We've been touched by what you've shared today," she went on, "and we'd like to know: What good could possibly come from this?"

In my memory I pause and pray silently for guidance. The last thing Kate needed was pious platitudes about silver linings, however theological they might be.

"Kate," I said after a moment, "you must feel so betrayed."

She nodded.

"Your husband has broken your trust, your friends have let you down—"

"And my church has too," Kate said, opening up. "They haven't known what to do, so have left me to fend for myself."

"It must feel difficult right now to trust anyone at all."

"It does," she said, wiping away a tear.

And that's when I remember it coming—a nebulous thought that crystallized into a light and clear insight.

"Kate," I ventured, "what if you were to treat this betrayal as a challenge to be fulfilled—learning how to rebuild trust after it's been so badly broken. What if you were to face that challenge with God and document your experience—the highs, the lows, the lessons learned as you rebuild. Do that and I can see you helping others rebuild trust after their own betrayals someday."

Kate became thoughtful and her face began to soften. "That might be something," she said. And there hope had been born that even this might birth something good.

DJ and I reach the terminal and wait for the next ferry, my mind returning to the bay. Those sandy words will be complete now, their meaning emerging from the mud.

Service born of suffering. Fruitfulness from lack. Divine life flowing through the cracks. Adversity can release our greatest gifts into the world.

Bringing healing.

Bringing hope.

Birthing life.

CHAPTER 9

GIFTS AND GRACES

Dear Sheridan,

I stumbled upon your book *Resurrection Year* a few months ago and have since given copies to family and friends. Thank you for voicing the feelings I've had in the face of my own disappointments.

My broken dream has been missing out on a teaching job I spent years working toward. The worst part has not been the rejection by the principal, or the shock of teachers and parents who believed I was a shoo-in for the role. It's been my feelings of confusion and anger toward God. I truly believed he was leading me to devote my life to teaching. I worked hard to complete my degree, gave my all as a teaching assistant for six years, and watched others with fewer qualifications waltz into classrooms straight out of college. The job went to someone younger. I think teaching is a dream I must let go of now.

I live in a small town. I can't go anywhere without being asked by a former student or their parents where I'm teaching now. This can be a humiliating reminder of what I'm not able to be. The beginning of the school year is difficult—the smell of pencils and markers in the stores, school supplies everywhere you look. I'm volunteering at an animal shelter and serving as a court advocate for abused and neglected children, so I'm trying to focus on others. But I still struggle to know if God has any plan for my life.

Thank you for your writing. I hope to see you speak in person one day when you next come to the southeast of the United States.

Sarah in Tennessee

I rush down the narrow stairs of the guesthouse, my backpack bumping against the wall. "Sorry I'm late. I was checking e-mail."

"No problem," DJ says. "We just need to pay the bill."

I settle up with the guesthouse owner, my face reflecting in the window behind him—eyes dark and hollow, patchy stubble on my cheeks and chin. I look rough now. We say good-bye to the owner and step outside.

"Day seven!" DJ says as we start walking. "Only two days to go."

I wonder to myself what could ever curb DJ's innate cheeriness. Not blisters, which I know have gotten worse for him these past two days. Maybe food poisoning. No—I saw him suffer that in the Philippines once, and he still managed a smile.

"To Bede's World!" he exclaims.

DJ has planned in a visit to a local museum dedicated to another northern saint, Bede, Britain's first historian.[1] Without Bede we'd know little of Cuthbert, Aidan, Oswald, or, indeed, much of England's origins.

If I'm honest, a museum trip isn't high on my agenda. We have miles left to walk. But why dampen things?

We pass a school and a cemetery, cross a train line and a freeway, and arrive at the museum as the doors open. A modern building with a white interior, it has Anglo-Saxon timelines on walls, glass cabinets with archaeological finds, life-size models of monks at work, and a sculpture of Bede, robed and seated, beckoning us in.

The museum's rooms are each themed to a different facet of the man. There's Bede the Historian, compiler of the monumental *Ecclesiastical History of the English People*, one of the most important records we have. There's Bede the Scholar, author of forty-plus books on music, poetry, nature, and grammar, along with dozens of biblical commentaries. A whole floor is dedicated to Bede the Scientist. A keen astronomer, Bede was the first to see how the sun, moon, and earth interact to change tides and seasons. A mathematician, too, he calculated a date for Easter that's still in use today,[2] and changed our calendars by introducing the concept of BC and AD.

I walk over to a cabinet. It holds a ceramic chalice with a woven cord etched around the rim. Beside it is a rectangular wooden board no larger than a hand, engraved with five crosses. It's a portable altar. In the early days when few churches had been built, traveling priests used apparatus like this to share the sacraments.

Unlike Aidan or Cuthbert, Bede rarely left home. Instead, he spent his days reading, calculating, and scribbling within the monastery's walls, venturing out only to check stories and sources. "My chief delight has always been in study, teaching and writing,"[3] he confessed—a patron saint for nerds everywhere.

A craftsman sits at a table, making silver jewelry with ancient Celtic tools. I wander over to watch. On the way I look around to see where DJ is.

He's with Bede the Scholar, looking thoughtful.

⸻

"And in here," the volunteer guide says, "through this archway, is the original church."

"Original, as in, *original* original?" I ask for clarity.

"Yes, indeed. Bede would have worshipped in this very room."

We stand in the chancel of a church downhill from the museum. This is St. Paul's Church, one of Britain's oldest buildings, center of the famed Jarrow Abbey where Bede spent most of his life. Now a small part of a larger building, this chancel was the original church built in 682. Here Bede penned his books by quill and candlelight. Here he prayed and preached and sang.

"See that small stained window up there?" the guide says, pointing. "The glass was made in the monastery. It's the oldest colored glass in the world."

"They made stained glass here?" I say, surprised.

"In the workshop by the river," she says. "The world's oldest intact copy of the Bible was crafted here too. You may have seen a replica in the museum."

I had. The Codex Amiatinus, a seventy-five-pound tome of over one thousand vellum pages handwritten in uncial script, had quickly caught my attention. Made just a few years before the Lindisfarne Gospels, it showed the unique Celtic-Germanic-Roman style they shared in its early development.

"That style was forged here in Jarrow," she says, "in the scriptorium. That's where Bede's books were copied by hand too. They were quite in demand."

We head outside. The ruined walls are from a later time, but an outline of the original monastery has been traced on the ground with bricks. To the right was a kitchen with an adjacent room for meals; to the left, a hall where the school and scriptorium were probably based. By the river, near the workshop, was a guesthouse for visitors. And tucked among it somewhere was the library, one of the finest of its time. I imagine Bede hurrying there each morning to immerse himself in the works of Pliny or Augustine.

Jarrow Abbey was founded by Benedict Biscop, a monk with a vision to build a model monastery for England.[4] He traveled throughout Europe collecting books for the library, securing artwork for the halls, contracting masons to fashion its stones. Scenes from the Gospels adorned the walls; friezes were carved with birds and vines, making Jarrow's simple buildings not just functional but beautiful. For two centuries this was Europe's leading center of scholarship and art. Then the Vikings came.

A modern sculpture hangs in St. Paul's near the entrance to the chancel—a wood carving of Christ ascending to the sky. There he hovers, just above us, arms outstretched, cracks in his wrists, a soft light making his cruciform body glow and his narrow face seem serene. It strikes me as a work of knotty, earthy glory.

I take one long last look before we leave.

Bede and his monastery evoke pride in these quarters. There are streets named Monksway, Abbotsway, Paulsway, and Pilgrimsway, and there's even a Bede Industrial Estate. A twelve-mile path called Bede's Way links Jarrow Abbey with its sister house in Monkwearmouth. We cross the road and step on.

"You know," DJ says, "I'm surprised by how emotional I was back there."

"Yeah?" I say. "Over what?"

"The faithfulness of those early believers and the heritage they left. It's strange—I'm from the opposite end of the world to them, there's thirteen hundred years between us, yet somehow I felt connected to them, as if I shared their spiritual DNA."

The Bede's Way path begins in a nature reserve then runs along the River Don. We move along its winding line through rustling trees under a calm white sky.

"Maybe some of what I felt is genealogical," he says. "My family tree is largely Irish and Scottish and, as a white Australian, there's a British link there, too, through settlement. But it's more than that. Many Western churches trace their origins to Britain, including the Anglican and Baptist churches that have most shaped me. They sprang from soil first sowed by people like Bede and Biscop. Standing in the museum, and then in the church, I felt like part of one big puzzle that connected us all.

And I felt a debt of honor to them. Without the risks they took bringing the gospel here, would I even be a Christian? My faith ultimately links back to theirs."

I think on DJ's words. That present-day Christians have gained from the sacrifice of these saints is clear enough. We walk in the light of their long-extinguished stars; we climb the boughs of the oak seeds they planted. But to imagine our personal faith as directly traceable to them, as if we're descendants on their family tree . . .

"That's a profound thought," I say.

We pass under a freeway and into another leafy reserve, take a small bridge across the river, and walk on its east side. My thoughts, too, have been on the legacy of those monks, although from a slightly different angle.

"We owe a lot to the monasteries they built too." As history tells it, those monastery guesthouses became the forerunners of our hospitals, and the classes in those halls the beginning of our schools. Universities like Oxford grew out of monks tutoring pupils, while the early scientists, like Bede, made their findings within monastery walls. Monasteries were early pharmacies, dispensing herbal and other remedies. They sprouted homes for orphans, the mentally ill, and the aged. It's even been said the scriptorium saved the great ideas of civilization from being destroyed. When barbarians razed medieval Europe, it was the classical books copied by the monks that survived.[5]

"And don't forget the wine," DJ says.

"Or the music," I add.

With their need for supplies, not the least for Communion, European monasteries became producers of fine wines, beers, and cheeses. And as for music, the Western song got its tonal structure from the Gregorian chant created by monks for prayer.

"Praise be to the monastery for beer, Bach, and brie," I say, smiling.

We follow Bede's Way along the shallow valley that cradles the river, suburban homes tucked neatly in cul-de-sacs on either side of us.

"I guess the other thing that moved me," DJ says, "was Bede himself. Aidan and Cuthbert were preacher-apostles, traveling the land calling people to believe. But Bede was a man of books and ideas—a theology geek like me! And his vocation was just as important as theirs. It felt like a validation of my calling as an academic."

"The scholar had a place, not just the evangelist," I say.

"What about you?" DJ asks. "Did anything at Jarrow resonate?"

We cross back over the river, zigging to its zag, then detour over a motorway before picking up the path again. I'm glad now that we visited the museum and St. Paul's. Something about them *has* spoken to me.

"The scriptorium," I say without pause.

I may not have seen the Lindisfarne Gospels yet, but I have gazed at copies of its pages—their stylized letters swirling with geometric patterns, with birds and flowers and interlacing vines; the calligraphic paragraphs intricate as lace with dashes of green and mauve filling the space between letters. It's a work of stunning artistry drawn with hand-mixed pigments and pens cut from goose feathers.

"And it came not from some bohemian art studio," I say, "but from a monastery. It's that embrace of the arts that has spoken to me. Imagine a church today with artists and scholars on its staff, not just priests or pastors."

I feel a stitch of frustration rise as I speak, a current annoyance of mine being roused. While Scripture points to the Spirit of God giving an astonishing array of gifts to the church—from miraculous healing and supernatural wisdom, to creativity and the ability to organize or encourage[6]—from my experience each wing of the church seems to narrow the list down to a few favorites it expects all to possess.

"For evangelicals the favorites are evangelism, teaching, and missionary gifts," I say. "For charismatics they're healing, prophecy, and speaking in tongues. For liberals they're mercy and social activism for the marginalized. Each of these gifts is important, but if you don't have one of those favored by your wing you can feel out of place."

"Or you can try faking one to fit in," DJ notes.

As Bede tells it, the Celtic church was aflame with spiritual gifts, some of the most spectacular said to have been at work in Cuthbert. Trapped with companions in the snow one day, Cuthbert foretold where food would be found and when their trial would end.[7] He predicted a king's fall in battle and his unexpected successor, as well as his own retirement and date of death.[8] To these prophetic abilities were added healing gifts. Stories abound of him curing illness—from a young man comatose with fever healed through Cuthbert's prayers, to a woman released from demonic seizures at his command.[9] According to the legends, our Cuthbert was quite the Pentecostal.

But these impressive gifts weren't the only ones valued by the British church, as a delightful story of Bede's shows.

While Cuthbert worked wonders in and around Lindisfarne, a woman named Hilda was running a monastery in Whitby, southeast of Durham.[10] One day Hilda's farmhand, Caedmon, came to her shaken. He'd had a mysterious dream.

"Caedmon," a man had said in the dream, "sing me something."

An old and simple farmer already self-conscious of his lack of musical talent, Caedmon politely refused. "I cannot sing," he said.

"Nevertheless," the man urged, "you must sing to me."

"What must I sing?" Caedmon asked.

"Sing about the beginning of creation."

And to Caedmon's amazement, as the dream progressed, he, indeed, composed such a song—about the Maker of heaven creating the wonders of the world.

When Caedmon woke he found he could recall the song in detail. He told his foreman about the dream, who took him to see Hilda, who listened carefully to his experience before giving him a task: produce another song, this time based on a verse of Scripture. Caedmon returned the next day with a new song.

Recognizing Caedmon's gift, Hilda made him a monk and got her scholars to educate him. Each day he was tasked with writing new songs and poems. And each day, Bede says, Caedmon wrote words of such "sweetness and humility" they moved people to tears, to worship, and to conversion.[11]

"Bezalel and Aholiab were gifted by God to be master artisans," I say.[12] "King David was gifted by the Spirit not just to lead but to be a musician.[13] But I don't see many books on spiritual gifts today with chapters on art or musicianship."

"Maybe the Celts can teach us something there," DJ says.

Having disappeared for a time under roads and embankments, the River Don ripples out of a tunnel to meet us again. It streams through elbows and s-bends before wriggling out to open fields like a piece of discarded string.

"Notice how our experience of Jarrow has drawn us to different things," DJ says. "Me toward the scholars and you toward the artists."

It's an apt reflection, one I should note. It may even help me solve a riddle.

A few years ago I taught a course at a theological college. It was on a subject I loved with students ready to learn. I enjoyed presenting the content, and the students did well. But after two years teaching that course I was bored.

At other times I've had opportunities to move into management of radio, print, and other organizations. A guy once offered me such a job only to soon withdraw it. Having heard what made me tick, he felt management would bore me too.

"Here's the thing," I tell DJ. "When I've done spiritual gifts tests in the past, teaching and organizing have often come up strong for me. And yet there's always been something else in the mix that's made straight roles based on them a bad fit."

And what is that something else, Sheridan?

Yes, what is it? I wonder.

Why *have* I resonated with Caedmon and the scriptorium when I neither write songs nor paint? Why *do* I gravitate to the arts section in bookstores and watch documentaries on photographers and architects? Why have I felt frustrated sitting in board meetings before? Why does teaching the same thing grow dull?

Because I'm driven to make new things rather than maintain what is.

I am not only built to communicate; I am called to create.

———

No one knows if the monks of Jarrow and Monkwearmouth walked this exact path between the monasteries, although their following the river seems a good bet. It's quiet out in the fields, the suburban din softened, birds and breeze and the trickle of water our soundscape now, our crunching steps an echo of the monks' long ago.

"Did you ever see *Mr. Holland's Opus*?" I ask DJ.

"The film?" He strains his memory. "I think so."

"About the guy who dreams of becoming a classical composer but has to take a high school teaching job to pay the bills. There's a song in his soul he labors to compose, but the responsibilities of a family, the needs of his students, and an unexpected fight to keep his music department open leave little time to pursue it."

"I remember now."

"Thirty years pass and Glenn Holland retires, his department finally closed through budget cuts. His opus is finished but he knows it's too late—he never made it in classical music, he'll never get funding to perform it. He's spent his life teaching students who'll probably forget him while his real life's work will go unheard.

"After Merryn and I watched the film I couldn't contain my excitement. 'What a great ending!' I said. 'The way Holland's past students all gather in that auditorium! He's changed their lives more than he knows! And then they take out their instruments and start playing his opus! What a message about how one's life can impact others!' And you know what Merryn said?"

"What?"

"'They never make movies like that about statisticians.'"

We laugh.

"At first I was annoyed by Merryn's cynicism," I say, "but then I realized she had a point. Judging by the films we make and the people we celebrate, the world has its own list of favorite gifts. Like singing and performing—"

"And fashion design and sports," DJ adds.

"Then maybe medicine and teaching and other people-helping gifts. These talents get the airtime, the awards nights, the film scripts, while others go unnoted."

We pass under a disused bridge, a remnant of a defunct train line, and as we do I think of Mick, a friend of mine. Mick works on a converted rail ferry that now operates as a giant floating hospital. The ship sails to developing countries, giving free health care to the poor, treating thousands of people each time.

When the ship arrives in port and the TV news crews come, they naturally point their cameras on its medical staff. The work these volunteer medicos do *is* astounding—removing tumors and goiters, healing cataracts and fistulas, fixing cleft palates and resetting club feet. Sometimes a journalist will wander below deck to interview other crew members. But few do stories on the work Mick does.

Mick and his wife, Tammy, left good jobs to bring their family onto the boat. Mick has an MBA; he was a chief engineer in the navy and dropped two levels of seniority to join. Tammy was in logistics, a role she loved. They knew ship life would be demanding, requiring flexibility and sacrifice, but Mick admits he was still surprised when he heard where he'd been assigned to work: in the ship's sewage plant.

With more than six hundred people on board at any time, up to forty thousand liters of waste is produced on the ship each day. Managing this toxic material is serious business—gassing is a risk, and people could die. Without Mick tending the pumps, those cleft palates wouldn't get fixed. Without his efforts belowdecks the whole operation would shut down.

In a celebrity-driven age it's easy to applaud those on the top deck and miss those serving in the engine rooms. St. Paul wouldn't allow it—he said *every* gift is important, the least prominent roles being the most vital.[14] And with its workshops and scriptoriums alongside its chapels, perhaps there's no greater model for today's church to follow in this than the multifaceted monastery of old.

"A spiritual gift is given to each of us so we can help each other."[15]

"Each person is given something to do that shows who God is."[16]

And whether it's working a miracle or calculating planetary movements, speaking angelic languages or writing songs that wrench a tear, curing illness with a prayer or making stained-glass windows, every gift and grace has a place in the community of God.[17] He makes some to be apostles, evangelists, and prophets, and others to be scholars, statisticians, and poets. While some part their lips and bring forth revelations, others are given the gift of making sewage systems work.

This is a message I've known but been slow to believe. For too long, deep down, I have felt inadequate, even jealous, watching those with gifts I don't have. If your car breaks down, I'm not the best person to call—if only I were more practically gifted. I haven't led thousands to faith, or seen many healings flow through my hands—if only I were a person of miracles. But if it's the Spirit who decides which gifts we get, there comes a time to accept his decision.[18] The gifts we have are given for a reason—to reveal God and help others in ways that are uniquely ours.

So here is my conviction, my new resolution: I will embrace the gifts I have, not fret for those I lack.

As a tool fits a task, so my gifts reveal my calling. I will follow them to my assignments and step in their direction.

It's dusk by the time we reach our motel at Roker, a neat seaside town of terrace homes and hedges with a long, curved pier arcing into the North Sea. We arrive to a steel sky with an apricot horizon, a lighthouse blinking on the water.

Our pace had slowed after crossing the fields. Stepping off Bede's Way for a more direct route along the roads, our feet grew sorer with every mile, our last three hours more difficult. We rest in the motel before heading out to dinner, spreading our maps on the table to plan tomorrow's walk. Our last day's trek will get us to Durham. Monday morning we see the Gospels. That afternoon we'll be heading home.

Back at the motel I type an e-mail:

Dear Sarah,

Thank you for writing to me. I was both touched by your words and saddened at your losing that teaching opportunity.

I take it you're settled in your town and wouldn't move for the right job elsewhere? I can imagine how hard those "Where are you teaching?" questions must be.

I wish I had something to say that would fix the situation. All I can share is what I'm starting to learn—that these seasons of confusion can be pivot points in our lives, shaping our characters, teaching us things we might miss otherwise. For one thing, this moment presents your best opportunity to discover who you most deeply are. Your career plans may have stalled but you are still a child of God. I hope this grounds your life in a fresh way.

I was moved to read about your advocacy for those children. I can imagine your impact in their lives, however difficult to make, being something God brings up when you meet face-to-face. Your animal shelter work is significant, too—it's Genesis 1:28 in action.

And I'm convinced of this: that if God has gifted you to teach—if it flows in your bones and you're effective doing it—then *you are a teacher* whether you have an official role or not. Who else in your community needs your gift? I'll be praying for a place where their need and your talent can meet.

Do let me know how you go.

Sheridan

CHAPTER 10

PATHWAYS AND PROVIDENCE

Inside one of my parents' old photo albums is a yellowing picture of a small boy in his first year of school. He has a roundish face with freckles on his nose, his straight white hair parted on the left. He wears a wide-collar shirt that sits skewed, and his gray corduroy trousers are short in the leg. This kid loves spaghetti, jelly, and ice cream sandwiches. He hates pumpkin, avocado, and peas. He owns just one record, ABBA's *Arrival*, but cartoons are more his thing. He could watch Scooby catch the ghouls and Wile E. Coyote with his dynamite all day.

There are other photos in that album—of pets and holidays and family events, and a few rare pictures of a teenager. His face is long, not round; his dark-blond hair is wavy, not straight. He has no freckles, likes avocado, watches movies rather than cartoons, and would never admit to owning an ABBA record. He spends weekends spinning club music in his bedroom, hoping to one day be a DJ. There's a competition coming up if he can only muster the nerve to enter it.

The small boy and the teenager are little alike. They have different tastes, aspirations, and understandings of the world; different skin, different teeth, different blood, different bones.[1] The boy riding his bike over the hills has memories the teen no longer recalls, while the teen will soon find courage the boy knows nothing of.

At the physical, emotional, and cellular levels those two boys are different people, even though they share the same DNA and go by the same name—even though they are both me. And they are different people again from the man now walking to Durham. Our existence is a profound mystery.

We humans are a paradox of change and continuity, billboards of changing colors in ever-resizing frames. And this paradox raises questions about our identities: Who are we really? Which one is the real us?

The person we once were, the person we are now . . .

Or the person we one day will be?

———

Sunday morning. Our last day of walking. The forecast: warm and bright. The early sky reminds me of my first days on Lindisfarne—a fluffy blanket of cloud hovering low, liquid silver sea caressed by fingers of orange light. We walk along the beachfront past the arcing pier, our final trek begun, this time with company.

News of our pilgrimage has reached Monkwearmouth, and

in an act of hospitality, DJ and I have been invited to a church service to be prayed for as we finish our trip. The service over, Paul, one of the ministers, now walks us to our first stop.

"Do you have children, Paul?" DJ asks.

"Three," Paul says, "and number four is due any day."

Conception. Such a marvel. One sperm out of millions meets one egg out of thousands from one moment of love between two people, who chose each other from thousands of potential partners, themselves products of one unrepeatable melding of two others born because their own parents happened to meet at that party or sit on the same train. One different sperm, one cross word, one missed party, one detail changed in generations of ancestry, and you and I wouldn't be here.

"Have you found out the sex?" I ask.

"Yes, we're having a little girl."

One unique body, one matchless face, its features drawn like a collage of leaves from the family tree—Dad's nose, perhaps, and Mum's lips, maybe the chin or hair from a great-grandmother somewhere—that unique body and face born into a bloodline that gives it an ethnicity, a nationality, a race.

And this little one, even now, unborn, is a *someone*. For she is already a daughter and a sister and a grandchild and a niece in the fabric of relationships she's woven into. She is infant, female, a cousin, too, and soon a friend, a neighbor, and a citizen. Paul's little girl will enter this world with a raft of pre-given identities.

"And the pregnancy," I ask, "how has that been for your wife?"

"To be honest," Paul says, "it's been stressful."

The esplanade ends at a small café and a block of change

rooms, and the three of us follow a connecting path around toward a quiet marina.

"At our twelve-week scan," Paul says, "Miriam and I were told the baby had a high nuchal measurement. At twenty weeks they told us she was extremely undersize and had a serious heart defect. The baby will need intensive surgery once she's born, and all the signs are pointing to her having Down syndrome."

Deep breaths and condolence sounds, words hard to find.

"We've been told to 'reconsider' the pregnancy so many times, or to at least do the tests to confirm Down's. We've always said no—what would it achieve? But they've often reminded us how most people terminate in these circumstances, how difficult life will be for both her and us if we continue, that we can always try again for a 'normal' child. Late-term abortion is still legal for Down syndrome in the UK. It's the path everyone has expected us to take."

"No wonder it's been stressful," I say.

"We've faced surprise, even disdain, for keeping her."

One sperm, one egg, one moment, one face—one special smile, cute giggle, unique voice and gait. A personality in a body with limits and capacities, quirks and tics and abilities to unfold. A body with a soul, a God-given riddle, full of talent and humor, joy and wonder, a sacred little girl, a divine image-bearer, born into a moment of time with all its possibilities and prejudices.

After the marina the footpath curves along a tree-lined street as the sun lifts and the cars come out. DJ tells Paul a little about Bethany's condition, I share something of Merryn's and my story, and as we walk flags appear on lampposts with directions to St. Peter's Church, the sister house to St. Paul's in Jarrow.

"The entrance is up here," Paul says as we approach a large green with an old stone church at its center. As we walk into the grounds my thoughts wander.

What a wondrous thing our existence is. Mine. Yours. The baby Miriam carries. A once-only threading together of genes and experiences sparked with a soul by the finger of God. How myopic, then, to reduce our identities to one thing alone, like a job title. Our complex selves are bigger than that. We are breathing, blinking miracles.

⁓

Our goal is to reach Durham Cathedral by 3:30 p.m. for its evensong service. That leaves little time to see St. Peter's. A small museum inside tells its story, how Benedict Biscop built it a few years before St. Paul's and how a seven-year-old Bede was one of the first pupils through its door. A calligrapher sits at a table making a copy of John's gospel as the scribes did long ago, and people soon start filing through the church's archway. Thirteen hundred years later, St. Peter's still holds services.

Word of our pilgrimage has reached a local newspaper, and soon a journalist named Keith arrives to get the story and take photos of us outside the church. Perhaps we say it outright or maybe he reads it on our faces, but his headline later is apt: "Monkwearmouth Churches Welcome Weary Pilgrims."

Weary we are. As Keith drives off, DJ sits down to remove his boots, revealing soles now fully covered in blisters. My back hurts, my hips ache, and I notice my legs shake when I stand still. And today's trip has hardly begun.

The early service and interview have put us behind schedule. With fifteen miles to go we'll need to make up time, fast.

This journey will be one we will never forget.

But thank God it's nearly done.

———

Aside from occasional visits to caves or inland detours around rivers, our pilgrimage to this point has stuck largely to the coast. But now we head southwest, leaving sea for soil on our descent to Durham. We step off, forcing our feet into rhythm.

"I've been thinking about Biscop and the impact he had," DJ soon says.

"Starting these churches, you mean, and training Bede?"

"Who would Bede have become without Biscop's input?" he says. "And yet how many people have heard of him? Biscop is a forgotten saint."

"It makes you wonder how many others we've forgotten too."

I had begun thinking along these same lines after one of my practice walks. Heading out along Oxford's High Street one Friday, I had passed Magdalen College, where C. S. Lewis once taught, and the deer-grazed grounds where he and J. R. R. Tolkien would wander and talk. I hiked up Morrell Avenue then took a maze of backstreets and paths to reach Holy Trinity Church where Lewis is buried.

While churchyard signs pointed the way, the grave had taken a while to find. I had crisscrossed the cemetery, stepping carefully but fast past headstones bearing the wrong names, before finding a white slab etched with a cross and epitaphs to

Clive Staples Lewis and his brother Warren. There I had stood quietly before taking a photo—Lewis's epitaph in the frame, Warren's cropped out.

Sitting later on a bench nearby, a thought had come: *Do you see what you have just done?*

How quickly had I sidestepped those other graves. How easily had I clipped Warren from the picture. Was he always the cropped-out one, always sidelined when Lewis was around? How many "nobodies" had I ignored in my rush to reach a "somebody"? Yet each grave held a somebody to someone.

Each one held the remains of one who had been a universe of hopes, fears, longings, and dreams, of memories, heartbreaks, doubts, and beliefs, of joys, battles, failures, and victories, leaving their own contribution to the world, however small. Who knows but one of those graves didn't hold a Cuthbert or an Aidan too? I just wouldn't have known it.

And what made C. S. Lewis such a celebrity to me and others anyway? His unfettered imagination and intellect for sure, bringing an Aslan, a Screwtape, an Elwin Ransom to life while being capable of a *Mere Christianity* too. But exceptional though he was, Lewis's life and work could have faded from history had a few dedicated friends not labored to keep it there—something other fine writers have missed out on.[2]

Many more leave their mark than are ever remembered, I reflect.

We approach the old Wearmouth Bridge to cross the River Wear. A plaque says it was first built in 1796 and has been replaced twice since. What other changes these banks must have seen—huts replaced with barns, then buildings of brick and glass, mules swapped for carts, then trams and cars—the surface of this earth changing over the years like an old table set again and again.

"What does it mean to glorify God?" I ask.

The question sounds random but to my mind follows our last conversation.

"You know," I add, "'man's chief end is to glorify God and enjoy him forever.'"

"The old Westminster Confession," DJ says.

"I've always liked the 'enjoying God' bit, but the first part seems nebulous to me, the thing everyone says without really knowing what it means."

DJ chuckles. "I have other problems with that line."

"Really?"

"It centers on us too much."

"Well, it *is* a statement of humanity's purpose—"

"But we do nothing without God acting first," he says. "We only know God because he first revealed himself to us. We only love God because he first loved us. We only glorify God after he's first made us his own. Everything starts with him, not us."

I wonder if DJ isn't being a tad pedantic, the fatigue of these miles showing in theological pickiness. But I soon see he's touching something true.

From the first word that brought the skies into being, made the seas churn, and the first creatures spawn, we have never been the center of this story. Born though we are of divine breath, loved into being as echoes of angels, we are mere notes in a great symphony that's been rising in pitch since creation's first day. Each of its movements plays out in history—from floods and rainbows to wandering tribes, from mountaintop revelations to weeping exiles, from cries on crosses and empty tombs to the great cadence when all heaven shouts in triumph—each of us a pluck of a string or a cymbal crash in God's great score. We aren't the ones holding each atom in place. We don't make the galaxies twirl. We haven't sacrificed all to bring humanity to wholeness. DJ is right. It all starts with God.

Our next stop is Chester-le-Street, an important one for the trip. At our current pace it's still three hours away. And DJ has again started to limp.

"With that in place," I concede, picking at the question again, "what does it mean to glorify God?"

I know the theology—that God's glory is the eye-watering brilliance of his being, his power and beauty brighter than a million suns, his goodness glowing in the person of Jesus, a radiance we're designed to reflect.[3] It's the *action* I'm thinking about.

"Of course, it includes praising God for who he is," I say.

"And giving God credit," DJ says, "like a singer recognizing the source of his or her gift."

"I'm coming to think glorifying God is about revelation," I say, "us revealing something of God's character through what we say and do."

Our gospel reading from yesterday morning has been on my mind. We had read John 17, Jesus's great prayer for his followers before his crucifixion, which speaks of how he has glorified the Father in various ways:

"I have revealed you to the ones you gave me . . ."[4]

"They know that everything I have is a gift from you . . ."[5]

"I brought glory to you . . . by completing the work you gave me to do."[6]

And the big one: "Glorify your Son so he can give glory back to you," meaning the cross, glory revealed through sacrifice.[7]

And it strikes me then that those who do the same—who give a glimpse of the unseen God through their sacrificial lives, who complete the tasks he's given them to do, playing their part in the symphony while pointing all attention heavenward—may be as great in the eyes of God as the most famous of writers or celebrated of saints, even if their names fade from history and vines crawl over their graves.

We walk for some time through the suburbs, feet heavy, soles raw. When we come to a bus stop I take the opportunity to drop my pack and get my water bottle, while DJ sits down and checks the time.

"We need another shortcut, don't we," I say resignedly.

"I don't think we have a choice."

I start searching the bus timetable for a mention of Chester-le-Street, and as I do a Subaru wagon pulls up with camera gear in the back. It's Keith, the journalist from this morning. He winds down his window to speak.

"I know you're on a pilgrimage, but do you two need a lift?"

We drag our bags from the back, wave Keith good-bye, and step toward the high-steepled church he's dropped us by. The sign out front reads, "Parish Church of St. Mary and St. Cuthbert. Founded AD 883." An old wooden door leads into a sanctuary of red carpet and high arches, a man in a suit walking up the aisle.

"I'm sorry," he says, "we're just about to lock up."

No problem, we say, and turn to leave, but on seeing our packs he asks where we're from. His name is David, we discover, and he's the vicar of this historic church at Chester-le-Street. Soon he's taking time to answer our questions.

"Cuthbert's coffin would've rested over there," he says, "in what is now the nave."

"In a wooden hut," I confirm.

"That's right. I don't think they expected to stay so long."

After pushing his coffin with its precious relics around the country for seven years, Cuthbert's monks found respite here when a local king gave them an abandoned fort. They built their church from sticks, probably thinking another run from the Vikings was near. Instead, they stayed here 112 years.

"This is an important place for the Lindisfarne Gospels too," DJ says.

"It was here that Aldred the monk added his Old English translation to each page," David says. "You can see it over here."

David takes us to an open cabinet. A few years ago the church raised money to have a complete facsimile copy of the Lindisfarne Gospels done, one of only two replicas in existence. It lies open in the cabinet, and David points out Aldred's fine handwriting between the Latin verses on a page of Mark's gospel, then moves aside for us to see.

"I'll give you a few minutes to look around while I check the doors," he says, "then I'm afraid I must get to a meeting."

DJ turns the sheathed pages carefully and soon comes to Luke. Its opening spread is dazzling. On the left page a stylized cross outlined in blue and filled with fine yellow interlace sits on a mass of orange, blue, and yellow diamonds like a vibrant Persian rug. On the right, a large Q—the first letter of Luke's first sentence in Latin—dominates the page. Outlined in black, the body of the letter is sectioned into small compartments, each filled with a scene. In one, two birds hook beaks while their talons fill the frame. In another, doglike creatures intertwine in a figure-eight pattern. There are peacocks, trumpets, spirals and scrolls, a swirl of red, mauve, lime, and gold that could command hours of attention if we had them. This will be the closest we come to handling the Lindisfarne Gospels, the real one kept secure in a glass box. If only we had more time.

I take a photo of the nave just before David returns. He's held two church services already and has a third coming this evening. This ancient church is thriving.

"One more question," I ask him. "What are those?" I point to a row of tombs along the wall, each with a chivalrous-looking effigy lying in rest, their faces worn smooth and a hand or foot missing from age.

"Those are fakes," David says. "A benefactor of the church had them carved to look old to make his ancestors seem important."

"When was this?"

"1595. They're now *historic* fakes."

We laugh at this stunt of manufactured significance, thank David for his time, and leave through that old wooden door.

⌒

A path leads around behind the church, under a freeway, and back to the River Wear.

"This is it!" DJ says, enthusiasm breaking through his exhaustion again. "The last leg of the journey."

"Time to man up!" I say.

Manning up has become a running joke on the trip about the last miles of each day demanding extra stamina. The number of man-up miles has increased daily with our declining energy. These last eight are going to be tough.

Warm and bright, the forecasters said, and true enough. We approach a park ringing with the squeals of children, its swings and slides full, a happy queue at the ice cream van. A bevy of swans squawk for their bread at the riverside while others move serenely on the water. It's the kind of day when you could believe that every part of creation glorifies God in its own way—the breeze in its lightness, the ground in its constancy, the gliding swan in its graceful ease, each tree lifting its arms, every tweet a chorus.

Whether the monks felt this way as they walked here, who knows. When the Vikings came again in 995, a new generation of Cuthbert's followers took to the road, pushing his coffin and the Gospels to Ripon and then Durham.

"According to the story," DJ says, "his body was supposedly incorrupt then, right?"

As Bede tells it, eleven years after burial Cuthbert's body was exhumed and found to have not decayed—the face still fresh, the joints flexible, like a man simply asleep.[8] This was said to still be his state when he was laid at Durham Cathedral in 1104, but a third check of his coffin in 1827 found only bones. This supposed miracle and the healings reported at his shrine spread Cuthbert's wonder-working fame far.

"All those healings are ironic," I note, "given he battled

chronic pain." During his early years Cuthbert contracted the plague, and, though apparently rescued through prayer, was left with a pain in his side for the rest of his life.[9] Cuthbert had been a wounded healer, divine life flowing through his frailty.

"I'm starting to wonder if there's a link between our ordeals and our gifting," I add. "Something special seems to happen when the two combine."

We take a road bridge across the river and the landscape turns agrarian. Over a stile and into a field we go, the turrets of a castle peeking above the trees.

I have been mulling this idea over since looking at the lives of great artists. When retinal disease began eroding his sight, Degas switched from paint to pastel because the chalk lines were easier to see. Renoir had to have brushes placed between his gnarled fingers when rheumatoid arthritis made them clench like claws. And when cancer surgery left him immobile, Matisse turned to collage, directing assistants where to attach each paper piece to a larger sheet fixed on the wall. The outcome for each was a creative breakthrough—Degas's *Blue Dancers*, Renoir's *Girls at the Piano*, Matisse's *The Sorrows of the King* and other masterpieces. The melding of adversity and ability birthed something new.

Something similar can be seen with other afflictions. Experiences of poverty and racism combined with poetic gifts gave Maya Angelou her powerful writing voice. The loss of a mother and a sister paired with a painter's gift made Mary Cassatt the definitive artist of the mother-child bond. With two wives lost as well as a daughter, his friends in prison, and his books banned, an old and blind John Milton dictated a novel that would shape the Western world's imagination for centuries. Would *Paradise Lost* have been as powerful without those trials?

Tracing the idea further, the pattern seems present in many of the faith leaders I've admired. Quadriplegia combined with a gift of encouragement has made Joni Eareckson Tada good news to those with disabilities. Incarceration plus a leadership gift helped Charles Colson reach prisoners around the world. A history in gangs plus an evangelistic gift has made Nicky Cruz a light to New York's streets. For these and others, the marriage of trial and talent has led to powerful service to others.

"Affliction plus gifting can make magic happen," I say to DJ.

I listen to myself and laugh a little inside. I could barely string words together for Keith's interview, weary as I was, and here I am getting deep with DJ about glory, gifting, and trials. It's the kind of conversation our friendship has always triggered.

"God uses our afflictions to shape who we are and what we do." DJ offers a summary. "That's a redemptive way to look at it."

We walk for an hour through fields and over hills, past farms and cottages, our conversation a distraction from our feet. If we ever do this again, we agree, we'll make more time for rest.

If there is a next time, that is. And I hope there is.

A dirt path leads into a wooded area, foliage sifting the sun to make a tunnel of leafy shadows. A series of steps takes us down to a river with a bridge across to more ruins. It's the Wear back to meet us again after various twists and turns.

We cross the bridge and find the ruins are of Finchale

Priory, a twelfth-century monastery founded on the hermitage of St. Godric. Once a sailor and merchant, Godric is said to have encountered Cuthbert in a vision and lived a life of prayer here for sixty years.[10]

It isn't the first posthumous appearance Cuthbert is said to have made. In fact, by the twelfth century he was apparently doing all manner of peculiar tricks from his celestial cloud—turning a thief into a fox, turning the Irish Sea into blood, using his staff as a rudder to guide a ship home, hitting houses with lightning, even striking people dead.[11] By then Cuthbert was more a Thor than Bede's kindly monk, his name exploited to secure Durham's power through the penances paid at his shrine.[12] No wonder later reformers such as Luther and Calvin wanted to tear those shrines down.

Godric seems sincere, though, with his simple ways and barefoot prayers. We wander through the priory, its bricks pocked and staggered, its roofless halls granular in their decay like dissolving sugar cubes.

A narrow road leads up a hill, gravity becoming our adversary. DJ puts his hiking pole to use, I push each knee to slog forward, and at the top of the hill, we check the map. It's 2:00 p.m., and we have five miles left. Evensong will be a stretch but still possible.

"What do you think you'll do after the PhD?" I ask, ready for more distraction. "If lecturing is the long-term goal, what comes next?"

"I guess I'll need to see how this work restructure goes," DJ says, "and what opportunities, or not, that brings. I'd definitely like to do more research at some stage, maybe into children and suffering."

Intellectual gifts illuminating an affliction he knows. That seems right to me.

"It's one thing for us adults to talk about facing trials with joy because of the character they can produce," he says,[13] "but another to say that to a child facing war or cancer, when the effects can be so deep and long-lasting."

"Whatever good might come of it," I say, "we can't romanticize affliction."

"And any redemption we see of it now will only be partial."

The road widens as grass verges appear, the land turning flat and open.

"I think about you and Merryn," DJ continues. "You're starting to see your pain redeemed but you're still left without a child, and some days that loss will hurt. Bethany is precious to Lou and me just as she is, with all her joy and love, and caring for her needs has probably made us better people—more humble maybe, more empathetic to others. But I'd still fix Bethany's disability in an instant if I could. Maybe that shows I haven't come to full acceptance yet and have my own issues to work through. But whatever good God brings from suffering now, I believe full redemption is still to come."

"I know that some wonder if it's even right to talk about a child with a disability being cured, since the condition is part of who they are."

"There's a lot of debate about this," DJ says. "The modern medical approach sees something like autism or Down syndrome as a problem to be fixed, leading to debates about gene engineering, abortion, and other 'solutions.' Some react to that clinical view, saying we're all on a spectrum of physical and intellectual abilities, so why single out those at the lower end of the scale as having a problem? And from a Christian stand-point, a child with a disability bears the image of God as much as anyone. These and other arguments lead some to think that even in the new creation, someone with Down's may still have the condition because without it they'd be a fundamentally different person."[14]

"And what do you think?" I ask. "What are your hopes for Bethany?"

"My hopes for her are the same as for you and me," he says. "That in the age to come there will be a continuity of who Bethany is now with a radical change in her being, freeing her from disability just as I will be freed from my own incapacities. Bethany will be herself but *more* herself than she's ever been."

One sperm from millions, one egg from thousands. One unique body, one matchless face. The boy in that photograph, the child Miriam carries, little Bethany with her smiles, the two of us now each in transition from one self to another as a seed becomes a shoot becomes a tree. What will we become in the end? The answer is thrilling and mysterious. For those on the path of God, a part of his symphony, all we're told is that ultimately we will be like him.[15] Our body with his nature. Our personality but his character. Ailments gone, afflictions over. Gifts glistening. Sins taken away. Our faltering candle flame of virtue turned into a furnace of other-centeredness making us the God-shaped selves he's always intended.

Until that day, and to the extent we yield to it, we are being drawn toward that future self. Step-by-step we go, one notch of radiance to another.[16] Becoming more like him, and so becoming our true selves.

An hour on we turn onto a tree-lined path, the cool shade welcome. If we'd continued on, we'd have reached the delightfully named town of Pity Me. According to legend that's where Cuthbert's monks dropped his coffin and the saint cried, "Pity me!" in rebuke. I guess it was that or a lightning strike.

Our boots crunch the dirt as our path slowly descends, a patchwork of fields around us with sheep grazing on the hills. And as the trees start to thin, we spot a milky silhouette through the leaves. There in the distance is Durham Cathedral.

What awe it must have struck in early pilgrims unaccustomed as they were to skyscrapers. With its cloud-pricking spires and heaven-high tower it's a sublime sight.

But it sure looks more than a half hour's walk away.

We grit our teeth and quicken our pace.

"Is there a later service we could visit instead?"

DJ limps badly. I wince with each step. It feels like walking on bare bone.

"This is the last one for the day," he says.

"It wouldn't be the end of the world if we missed it . . ."

When 3:30 p.m. comes we have only reached the edge of town.

"We can slip quietly in the back," DJ says, still keen for evensong.

Cuthbert apparently expressed his wish to be buried here by causing his coffin to get stuck in the mud. He sure had an eye for real estate. Like a fairy-tale city, Durham is built on a hill in the loop of a river, the cathedral on top like a jewel.

We start making our ascent.

———

A footbridge takes us across the river and into a newer part of town. It feels silly asking directions in such a small city, but every deft turn will save time. We're pointed to a set of stairs leading up to a shopping center. From there we cross a street and enter a large paved square with a church on the corner, the city's heart.

"I guess we go left," I say as the street forks, the left path rising.

We rush now. DJ squints in pain as his hiking pole clacks on the street.

The street narrows and winds past banks, bakeries, cafés, and clothing stores tucked into neat brick shops with large wood-framed windows. Another fork to consider, the main street taken. I try to suppress the pain but a gasp escapes every few steps.

Past the barbershop, the bookshop, and the pub we go, boots thudding, pole clacking. And as we turn onto a small cobblestone street, DJ suddenly cries out in pain.

"Ah!" he says, limping to a stop.

Teeth bared, leaning on the pole, he lifts his right foot for relief.

"It must be a blister that's . . . burst."

———

I think of the swollen soles I saw this morning with their biscuit-sized blisters, and imagine with a shudder a red-raw wound now chafed by sock and flapping skin.

He only stops for a moment, though, before making a wary step forward, right foot restricted to the briefest touch of toes to ground.

We slowly gain speed again, the cobblestone path leading us up and right, the buildings on either side getting older as we climb, until we reach the top of the fairy-tale city and a large grassed square called the Palace Green. Museums and colleges dot its perimeter. Durham Castle stands guard behind us. And there before us, with its grand windows and its tower nearly seventy meters high, stands the jewel.

From here the cathedral's entrance looks like a mouse hole. As we reach it we find the doors are over four meters high. The left door is open. We step inside.

It's 3:42 p.m.

We're late. But we made it.

⌣

It's the quiet I notice first. The holy hush. A quietness punctuated with the soft, distant voices of a choir, their words hovering somehow like smoke you could waft with your hand. It isn't the vast vaulted ceiling that strikes me next, or the giant stone columns, or the grand rose window dappling color onto the floor. It's the sheer number of people I see. The cathedral is packed. There isn't a seat free.

Since when did evensong become so popular?

Desperate to get off our feet, we hobble behind the throng,

careful not to disrupt the hush or bump anyone with our unwieldy packs, to find the last surfaces suitable for backsides—the corners of two large, square column bases. I lean on one edge facing forward, DJ sits on the base opposite, facing back.

"A reading from Bede's *Life and Miracles of Saint Cuthbert...*"

A female voice echoing softly. How timely to arrive just as Cuthbert gets a mention. But then, he probably gets mentioned here all the time.

After the reading a scripture is recited, then a visiting bishop gets up to speak. Neither of us can see what's going on at the front. DJ scans the stained-glass window on the back wall while I gaze at the sky-high ceiling. Closing my eyes to rest, I zone out to the bishop's first words—until something he says wakens me.

"Some of you have been on a pilgrimage . . ."

I open my eyes. *Did I hear that right?*

I look at DJ but he's still lost in the back window.

"You have walked in the footsteps of Aidan and Hilda . . ."

DJ looks at me now.

". . . of Biscop and Bede . . ."

Curious smiles grow.

". . . and today you're here to honor St. Cuthbert, who is buried in this cathedral."

What's going on?

The bishop then recounts Cuthbert's life—how he ventured into places others avoided, how he prayed till his tears fell, how he preached up a storm, how he was humble and gentle, a man of mercy and miracle, a hermit at heart but obedient to any call, an example we can all follow—just as DJ and I have learned.

It feels like a setup, something orchestrated just for us. Did someone tell them we were coming?

When the final hymn ends, I ask an attendant what just happened. "It was a service dedicated to Cuthbert, Bede, and pilgrimage," she says.

"Do you run these often," I ask, "or was it because the Lindisfarne Gospels are in town?"

"Neither," she says. "It was a one-off event."

And we just happened to stumble into it after walking in the steps of Cuthbert and Bede on our own pilgrimage. Sweet serendipity. God's sneaky surprise. Had we come a day earlier, or even twenty minutes later, the moment would have been missed.

It's the kind of experience that can get you wondering . . .

. . . wondering whether all the climbed trees and cart rides, the raided farms and school fights, the nervous waits for audition forms and knotted stomachs on contest nights, the letters that opened up careers, the dreams lost and the burnouts, the times the seals sang as we walked on water, the battles, the victories, the epiphanies in motel rooms, and all the other details found between the first wiggle of our hands and our final breath haven't been known from the start and somehow had their place.

It gets you wondering about a time when we stand among the faithful, hear a Voice say our names, and recount the highlights of our lives, and whether in that moment dots won't connect, pennies drop, and random threads be seen to tie.

It makes you wonder if we may then see that all the dead ends, wrong turns, scars, scratches, and blisters were somehow integral to the making of us.

Woven together under the gaze of Providence, crafting something good.

CHAPTER 11

A NEW CREED

We pull away so gently it seems as if it's the world outside that moves. Blue-striped poles slide past my window, then ticket gates, information screens, benches. When the last Durham sign flashes by and the platform runs out, the high vantage point of our viaduct-running track grants a full vista of the city—castle nestled among clouds of treetops, cathedral walls golden in the afternoon sun.

"Welcome to the 2:48 p.m. service to Reading," the announcer says, "stopping at Darlington, York, Sheffield, Birmingham, Oxford . . ."

I soak up my last view of the fairy-tale city. A few seconds later it's lost to trees. Within minutes we've wound our way above Durham's terrace houses, out past its suburbs, and into verdant hills and fields.

A lady soon appears with a refreshments cart. I buy some chocolate and lean my head against the window. And as the patchwork fields rush by with their hedgerow seams, I notice my weary relief mixes with another, stranger, sensation.

The pilgrimage barely over, it already feels like a dream.

———

The day had begun in search of a razor. Pulling my boots one last time onto feet that will hurt for weeks to come, I had wound down those same cobblestone streets to an all-hours supermarket for a pack of disposables. With another newspaper interview and our Gospels visit planned, it seemed wise to freshen up.

Not that we were particularly presentable. DJ and I sported the same quick-dry trousers we'd worn all trip, the same caps, the same jackets. I realize I'm wearing the same green T-shirt I first set out in, wrinkled from yesterday's hand wash.

Breakfast couldn't have been better—a "full English" of bacon, eggs, sausages, and hash browns leisurely enjoyed at St. John's College, a heritage-listed building in the shadow of the cathedral with ivy-covered walls, chesterfield couches, and a dining room overlooking tended gardens.

"The next station is Darlington."

And now I return home, thinking of Cuthbert as I do. I imagine him crossing those mudflats back to his island retreat after one of his busy missions, ready for a season of stillness. Surely such a rhythm is key to managing life's tensions, keeping rest and action, contentment and ambition, an acceptance of who we are with the drive to become something more all in balance. In my healthiest times I have lived to such a rhythm, sabbath rests punctuating my days, not just my weeks. More often than not I have charged through the seasons, one long expelled breath without an inhale.

Journey, return. Movement, stillness. Out, back, then out again.

I sink into my seat, let the train carry me home, feeling swept up in a rhythm of mission and retreat as the tides of Lindisfarne ebb and flow.

"Tickets, please," a conductor says, coming down the aisle.

DJ must be nearly home by now, his train having left earlier. After seeing the Gospels and meeting the reporter, we had said our good-byes with backslaps and man hugs, then he'd picked up his rucksack to return to Kintore—to beaming smiles and nursery rhymes, to doctoral classes and research papers, with insights about his aspirations tucked among his clothes. It will be a while before we see each other again.

"Going through to Reading, are we, madam?" the conductor says. "Well, I'm getting off at Birmingham. Would you do me a favor and lock the train before you leave?"

Laughter ripples through the cabin. North England is known for its comics and comedians, and evidently their train conductors carry the same gene.

"Anyone like venison? The supermarket has it on special this week. I thought about buying some but decided, no—it was still *too deer.*"

As I told the newspaper reporter this morning, it's that cheeky, chatty friendliness that's helped me fall in love with the North.

"Oxford!" he says now, punching a hole in my ticket. "Such a fine place. I'll be sure to visit you when my parole comes through."

After waving DJ off, I had set out on one last mission. Crossing the grassed square, I had approached Durham Cathedral's giant door and returned to the house of serendipity. It was now beautifully vacant apart from some milling tourists and a few prayerful souls, and I wandered down the center aisle as if to be crowned, passing columns as wide as I am tall, its rows of pews fading into the distance, to slip into a seat beneath that soaring ceiling and reflect for a while.

There I sat, gazing at the grand rose window a hundred meters ahead—Christ seated in the center, the twelve apostles around him, Revelation's twenty-four elders around them, in concentric swirls of prismatic color.

Thank you.

I had come feeling like a plastic bag caught in the breeze. A soul tossed by the forces. Searching for my *one big thing.* While I've made some discoveries, there is more clarity to find. I still want for a purpose I can put into a sentence. There has been no voice-from-heaven calling, no glittering new dream. But sitting there I felt grateful for all that had been—for the pilgrimage, for the moment, for the sense that all would be well. I also had a hunch I'd collected more answers than I realized. I just needed time to coax them out. Better get a new journal.

I slid out of the pew into the cathedral's south aisle, passed the marble pulpit with its shiny bronze rails, walked through the carved choir stalls and past the high altar, through archways and chapels with flickering tea-candle prayers to climb six small steps up to a narrow doorway. There I stepped onto a landing beneath the rose window, meters of stained glass soaring above me, to find four silver candlestands around a dark stone slab etched with just one word: *Cuthbertus*.

Here, after all the visions, predictions, and hilltop missions, all the tear-stained praises and sea-soaked prayers, after his befriending of monarchs, peasants, and paupers, his stomping through marram grass waging war with darkness, after all the fiery sermons, washing of feet, and cupping of sad faces in his hands, then a hundred years at the mercy of others becoming as much a myth as a saint, our hermit-monk had been laid to rest, the final stop on his own pilgrim path.

And at that shrine I wondered what Cuthbert's *one big thing* had been. A cathedral for his relics was far from his mind. The Lindisfarne Gospels were another's idea. None of the churches or schools named in his honor, or the histories written or pilgrimages in his name were ever in his heart to see. All these had spun out from the force of his life, eddies in the wake of his leaving. Cuthbert's vision had been the Composer and the great symphony, performing whatever part he was called to play.

Artists are judged by their body of work, not by one single painting or performance. And it seemed to me that Cuthbert's life would be judged in the same manner—not by its headlines alone but by the fine print in between. He rose in rank, saw thousands come to faith, became a counselor to kings and queens. But did any of these accomplishments outweigh the kiss placed on that fevered forehead?

Cuthbert's *one big thing* wasn't seeing monasteries built, movements started, or any grand plan achieved. His *one big thing* was the entirety of his life.

The great and the small of it given as an offering.

"Arriving at Birmingham New Street," comes the announcement.

We enter a series of brick tunnels on approach to the platform, pulses of darkness turning the windows into mirrors that reflect passengers farther up the aisle readying to leave. The train seems full for a Monday afternoon. I catch a reflection of my backpack in the luggage bay with my camera inside. I watch it closely as people go.

Cuthbert traveled lightly in this world, leaving few possessions behind him. This was confirmed as we queued at the university library, clutching our timed tickets to see the Lindisfarne Gospels. Dark inside with spot-lit exhibits, the library had also had other relics of Cuthbert's coffin on display. The most elaborate was a small gold cross found among his robes, inlaid with garnet and slightly damaged. The most modest was an ivory comb with one tooth broken, clearly owned by the saint, as why else keep it? There had been a small wooden altar like the one seen in Jarrow, some finely embroidered vestments, the oldest of their kind,[1] and even the remaining fragments of the coffin itself pieced together to show the engravings on its sides.

The monks had carried other precious things in that coffin: Oswald's head, Aidan's bones, a pocket-sized book with embossed leather binding. That book sat open behind protective glass, its pages yellowed but intact—Cuthbert's gospel of John.[2] It had lain on his chest near his heart where it belonged all those wandering years.

A book he touched, a comb he used, the coffin that carried his body. Seeing these things somehow compressed time, making the man of the stories tangible.

We had wound our way around the exhibition and its artifacts, following its corridors to a dimly lit room. And there at the end, in its climate-controlled box, in a V-shaped brace with a few small spotlights, was the marvel we'd come all this way to see.

It sat open at a picture of John the Evangelist. Seated on a throne with a scroll in his hand, an eagle above him carrying a book to heaven, John looked at us with a plea to have our names in the Book of Life. Red robe, blue cushion, an orange nimbus around his head—the colors were as rich as his eyes were piercing.

To guard them from light and other damage, each page of the Lindisfarne Gospels can be displayed for only a short time once every five years. How I wished I could reach in and touch that book, flip to Matthew's filigree-filled first page with its bass clef letters, or to the Chi-Rho spread abloom with twirling pink discs. Just one turn would get us to John's opening sentence— its bold black words filled with emerald and scarlet dashes and lined with fine red dots like the lights on an old cinema sign. Creatures chase and tumble within its letters, lilac circles whirl, dogs peek from corners. There are birds and vines inside fine gold frames, and in, around, and through it all, a labyrinth of interlaced lines ducking and weaving.[3]

Such detail, they say, could have taken a decade to complete, the whole of Lindisfarne involved—some preparing the vellum, others mixing the pigments, Eadfrith doing the artwork, Aethilwald sewing the binding, Billfrith crafting the jeweled case, every monk praying, that body-wracking work done in cold, wet huts in an age of war and plague. But this was a labor of love, a holy calling, every dot, dash, and stitch offered as a prayer. The Word was being enfleshed in a work of sacred beauty. It was only right to take time crafting it to last.

There's over a mile of elegant calligraphy inside that book, Aldred's scribbles fluttering between its rows like an editor's notes on a first draft. If you look closely you'll find an ink splash on one of the pages, words crossed out on others, even some question marks. Some letters are unfinished, some spots lack gilding, a wrong color has been used in Luke, someone has numbered the pages incorrectly. This magisterial work also has its blemishes. It is stained, imperfect, incomplete.

An artwork. An icon. A window to God. A masterpiece of pattern and word.

Complex. Priceless. Changing through time. Marked. Unfinished. Flawed. With its intricate design and dramatic story, that book caught my breath. And maybe the reason why went deeper than its beauty. Maybe it echoed something else.

Beautiful, tarnished, incomplete. Made to reveal God, made for eternity. With its winding lines like a pilgrim's journey, that book is us—all we are and will be.

⁓

Through rolling hills and winding streams we go, passing cozy towns with wafting chimney smoke, big-box stores, and busy factories as suburb and countryside converge. I watch dusk fall and the trees silhouette, the world turning amber and iron.

"Arriving shortly at Oxford station."

Interest in pilgrimage has grown in recent years, with even the nonreligious hitting the paths. Some go in search of meaning or "something more," others to leave a lost love, a lost dream, or an old life behind. The theme of relinquishment is unavoidable, particularly as a pilgrim returns home. At the end of the Santiago de Compostela route in Spain, pilgrims often burn their boots or throw something into the sea to symbolize their giving up the old for the new.

Relinquishment will prove an important theme for me, too, in the coming days. I will find that calling people to hand their dreams to God will help many to start again, sometimes in dramatic ways. At one church service in the future, hundreds of written dreams laid at a cross, a man will tap me on the shoulder.

"I don't normally go to church," he'll tell me. "I don't really know why I'm here. I was just walking past outside and something drew me in."

And what I said tonight about broken dreams . . .

". . . was exactly what I needed to hear."

Like you were meant to be here . . .

"It's as if I was meant to be here."

And I'll smile.

"Because tonight I was going to take my life," he'll say, wiping that smile from my face. "I was going to get blind drunk and step off a bridge. But I won't now," he'll add, "because now I'm a child of God."

Dark intentions relinquished for a new start.

And what will you relinquish, Sheridan?

The train slows as we approach Port Meadow and rows of homes now familiar to me after two years of residence.

Greed, pride, lust—there is always some sin to relinquish. But maybe it's the less obvious ones that now need picking from the cracks. Like comparing myself to others and the envy that brings, or fretting about my gifts, or worrying too much what others think. Or my secret desire to make a name and leave a mark, be acknowledged, be impressive. Or my fears about the future, or how many books I'll sell. Will I relinquish my desire for certainty and walk on in faith? Will I hand over my legacy, leaving it for God to make? Will I relinquish my bowerbird attempts to weave an identity from shiny things? Only God knows how much I will.

But, Lord, please know I want to.

"Oxford station, platform on the left."

Hoisting up my bag one last time, I step onto the platform and move toward the gates. Merryn says I should catch a taxi home—a fair indulgence after all these miles—but it only seems right to finish this on foot. I head outside and turn onto Botley Road, the day's last light a glow above the trees. Within a minute I'm crossing the old Osney Bridge over a silver-orange River Thames. Oxford sure is pretty.

It's a short walk home, about fifteen minutes. It will take a while longer to settle my questions, though. Three autumns and more will pass before I cross the bridge back one particular morning, heading to a café not far from where Shakespeare lodged, and take a table on the third floor. Sitting by a window I will slip on my glasses, open a journal, and try to fashion some words—a creed of sorts that might guide me forward, something to be read, reread, and dwelt on. After many scribbled phrases and crossings out, I will arrive at this:

The Creed

The hands that spin the galaxies brought me into
   being.
The one who holds the stars has made me his own.

———

I am God's child. My life is rich, my days are sacred.
>I have meaning and value.
>Even when the shadows fall.
I am held by a love that's wider and higher than the farthest edges of this expanding universe. My first task in life is to embrace this love.
>Leap into its depths.
>Splash in its waves.
>Drink it in.
>Let it define me.
>Seeking my worth in no other thing.
I am a pilgrim in this world, in search of wisdom and wonder.
>I will take new adventures.
>I will follow God into the unknown.
>I will listen for God's whisper.
>Knowing wrong turns will come.
>And that even then, I am still in God's hand.
Love is the river from which all the streams of life flow.
>I love God, I love others.
>This is my mission.
>Whatever my role.
What I achieve is not as important as the person I become.
>I will seek to imitate the Nail-Pierced One.
I will step in the direction of my strengths and talents.
>They are Spirit-given tools for my God-given tasks.
I will pay attention to my persistent aspirations.
>They could be the whispers of God.

I will serve all I can but walk deeply with a few.
>Brothers, sisters.
>Joy bringers, soul keepers.
>It is a holy thing to be called a friend.
The path is long and the terrain at times hard.
There will be tears, scars, and unfulfilled longings.
>But:
>The tears can take us deeper into the heart
>>of God.
>The scars can initiate us into a tribe we can serve.
>Through those empty spaces divine life waits
>>to flow.
>And so I will walk on.
I will step to a rhythm of mission and retreat.
>Each day, each week, each season.
I will aim for great things but leave my legacy to God.
>Knowing grace covers my failures.
I am one brief flash on the timeline of history.
Just one note in the great symphony.
>Still:
>I will not wish for another's life.
>I will take my place.
>Play my part.
>Something important will be missed if I don't.
For the hand that spins the galaxies wants me here.

I walk by St. Frideswide's Church, past the bicycle shop and convenience store, my feet wishing I'd taken the taxi. I've been away only twelve days, yet it feels as if I'm returning from months spent in a far country. Maybe in a sense that's true.

The interesting thing is that if life had gone according to plan I'd have never made this pilgrimage. What, then, of the discoveries that journal will hold? Perhaps when life as we know it ends, new adventures really can begin. Maybe when identity is lost we can discover who we really are. And maybe the adversity we despise can release our greatest gifts into the world. Providence has form in that regard.

I turn into our street and head for the blue door, the final bar of this pilgrim-song.

Another turn of the labyrinthine line.

Tomorrow it will wind somewhere new.

ACKNOWLEDGMENTS

What began as a tale about two friends on a walk became a four-year personal challenge when I realized more soul-searching would be required to write this book than I ever expected. Thank you, Daisy Hutton, Matt Baugher, Megan Dobson, and the whole Thomas Nelson team for your patience as I stumbled my way toward clarity.

The journey at the heart of this book started with a conversation. Over coffee one day, Joanne Cox-Darling mentioned that Peter Phillips from the CODEC Research Centre at St. John's College, Durham University, had an idea for a Lindisfarne–Durham pilgrimage route. I will always be grateful to Jo for the introduction, to Pete for the opportunity, to Bex Lewis and Emily Tamara for their help, and to David Wilkinson for the go-ahead to trial that route via a grant that enabled DJ and me to walk.

Thank you to the small band of friends who journeyed with me as I wrote: Allen Browne, James and Beth Campbell-Bruce,

Clare Bruce, Melanie Fielding, Jason Gor, Amy McGinnis, Graham and Rachel Quinlan, Jo Swinney, Tony and Vivienne Voysey, and Adam Walton, whose reflections helped sharpen the ideas of each chapter. After I then handed in what I thought was a seamless manuscript, Meaghan Porter spotted its missed stitches and frayed ends, while Jamie Chavez ironed out the grammatical creases. I'm grateful for such skilled editorial help.

Some names and details in the story have been changed to protect privacy, some events have been moved in time to aid clarity, and some additional conversations between DJ and me have been included to those had on the trip. This book isn't just the product of one retreat and pilgrimage, but four years reflecting on both.

Thank you, Merryn, for walking every path with me.

Thank you, DJ, friend and fellow pilgrim, for conversations that feed the soul.

Thank you, God, for every adventure.

Walk on.

REFLECTION GUIDE

CHAPTER 1: A SOUL ADRIFT

1. Reflect on your feelings after reading this chapter. Was there a scene or phrase that spoke to you in some way?
2. What did you want to do with your life in your twenties? Are you doing it now?
3. Think about the dreams you've had for your life over the years:

   Which have been *fulfilled*?

   Which are currently *unfulfilled* or even broken?
4. Sheridan describes feeling like a plastic bag floating in the breeze without direction. What image or metaphor would you use to describe your life right now?
5. Why do you think times of transition challenge our sense of identity and purpose?
6. Read at least two of the following biblical stories:
   - Moses at the Tent of Meeting (Exodus 33:7–11)
   - Elijah on the mountaintop (1 Kings 19:11–13)

- Anna in the temple (Luke 2:36–38)
- Mary sitting at Jesus's feet (Luke 10:38–42)

What do these people have in common as they approach God?

7. At the end of the chapter, Sheridan describes an experience of hearing God "speak" to him. How many channels are you open to hearing God through right now?

- Scripture
- Prayer
- Trusted Christian leaders and friends
- Dreams
- Prophecies
- Books like this one
- Other:

For help on discerning God's voice from other voices, see www.sheridanvoysey.com/tmoutools.

8. "Your first calling in life is to be with God." Reflect on this idea. How important do you think it is to recognize that our primary calling is to be with God, before any career or role? What weaknesses might an alternative approach bring?

CHAPTER 2: SAND AND STARS

1. Was there anything in this chapter you particularly related to? Note the ideas and themes that got you thinking.

2. What *Me's* have you wanted to be over the years? Which ones fit and which didn't? What did you learn from roles that didn't fit well?

3. How do you typically describe yourself when introduced to others? Why?

4. Do you agree that "a broken dream can shatter one's sense of self"?

5. Read one of these passages about God's presence revealed in creation:
   - Job 38–41
   - Psalm 19:1–6
   - Proverbs 8:22–32
   - Romans 1:19–20

   How can attending to creation help ground us during times of turmoil?

   For a practical exercise on contemplating creation, see www.sheridanvoysey.com/fivepractices.

6. "The same hands that made the galaxies crafted us in the womb." Read Psalm 139:1–18. What does it reveal about God's valuing of you?

7. "Until I let this love define me, I will forever seek my worth in lesser things." Read Ephesians 3:14–19.

   What "lesser things" do you define yourself by?

   How will you dwell in God's love instead?

8. "See how very much our Father loves us, for he calls us his children, and that is what we are!" (1 John 3:1). Can you say today that being God's child is more important to you than all other identities?

CHAPTER 3: CAVES AND CROSSROADS

1. What scene, phrase, or idea caught your attention in this chapter? Why?

———

2. It's easy to get discouraged when life goes wrong and then to give up, stop moving, and stagnate. If this has ever happened to you, describe when.

3. Read Matthew 7:7–8. Sheridan says this passage helped him learn to put action behind his prayers for guidance. What one thing can you do this week to move forward, adding action to your prayer?

4. Has fear of making a wrong decision ever held you back?

5. How can Proverbs 3:5–6 and Romans 8:28 help us make big decisions?

6. "Better to pray, seek counsel, make a choice, and walk forward, trusting God to correct any wrong turns we make, than forever wonder what might have been." Do you agree with this?

7. Both Sheridan and DJ see that key childhood experiences have shaped their values and concerns today. How has your childhood shaped you? Here are two exercises that may help reveal this:

   Recall a defining childhood experience and work forward. What was the event, why was it so memorable, and what convictions does it prompt as you recall it today?

   Pick something you're passionate about and work back. When did that interest first develop? What was the experience that first revealed its importance to you?

8. "Good things can come when you step into uncertainty." What faith step might God be calling you to make right now, however small?

CHAPTER 4: VISIONS AND WHISPERS

1. What in this chapter touched, moved, or got you thinking?
2. Have you ever had an experience of God clearly directing you to do something? What were the circumstances?
3. Looking back, have you been led by God without explicitly knowing it at the time?
4. Compare Cuthbert's calling (page 48) with Aidan's (pages 54–55). How do you see them being similar or different? How can this help in understanding God's guidance of us today?
5. "Maybe the path of one's calling is more a forest walk than a freeway." How does "straight-line" thinking manifest itself in your life? Has it ever stopped you seeing the significance of certain points along your journey?
6. "When I couldn't hear God's voice, I was still in his hands." How do you feel about this sentence?
7. Sheridan reflects on the passions and godly desires that have pursued him over time, seeing in them a source of potential guidance. Read Philippians 2:13.

    What passion or interest within you won't go away? (e.g., to paint, to be a mentor, to reach at-risk kids)

    What dream or aspiration has gently followed you over time?

    For more on discerning God-given dreams, see www .sheridanvoysey.com/tmoutools.
8. What opportunity lies open before you that you have the skills and energy to address? Could this opportunity be a God-given one?

CHAPTER 5: CASTLES AND ASHES

1. What is your response to this chapter? Did it prompt you to think further about anything in your life?
2. Recall Dunstanburgh Castle and the earl's potential motives for building it. What "castles" might you have built in the past to try to impress others?
3. Through the story of Chelsea, the famous interview guest, and recent experiences of his own, Sheridan explores various ways we try to make ourselves look important or significant to others. Which are you prone to?
   - Trying to impress others through your home, car, or clothes
   - Using brand names to project a certain status
   - Name dropping successful people you know or have met
   - Pursuing fame and public recognition
   - Reminding people of your accomplishments
   - Other:
4. On a typical day, which of these phrases best describes you:
   - I am what I own
   - I am what I achieve
   - I am what I earn
   - I am what others think of me
   - I am a child of God
5. Read and reflect on at least two of these passages:
   - Luke 15:11–32
   - Ephesians 5:1–2
   - 1 John 3:1–2

How does being a child of God give us significance and
security?

6. Imagine reading your obituary. What kind of
accomplishments does it say you achieved? Based on your
present use of time, are you heading toward such a legacy?

7. Imagine your funeral. Based on who you are today, what
kind of person are people saying you were? Is there
anything you'd rather they said instead? (Galatians 5:16–23
can be a helpful tool here.)

8. What will you regret not attempting before you die?

CHAPTER 6: RIVERS AND STREAMS

1. Review your response to this chapter. Write down any
phrase, story, or idea that got you thinking.

2. Where is "home" for you? Do you agree home is a place of
both belonging and becoming?

3. Who are your Herberts and Elfledas—the friends with whom
you can share your deepest joys, trials, hopes, and regrets?

4. Who is your Boisil—the mentor who calls you toward
God's purposes?

5. Which has greater priority in your life right now: work or
friendship? Is there a balance to regain here?

6. "We can't always do what we want to do, but doing what
we *need* to carries its own honor." Reflect on this in light
of previous generations. Do you think we ask too much of
work today, looking to it for a sense of self-fulfillment?

7. Read through John 15 slowly. Allow God to speak to you
through it today. What is he saying?

---

8. "There's only one real calling, whatever our job or career path—to love God and love others. That's it. Nothing more." How might your life feel different if loving God and others was your mission statement?

CHAPTER 7: THE SPACE IN BETWEEN

1. Did anything in this chapter resonate with a personal experience of your own?
2. Sheridan describes his experience of being initiated into a "tribe" after going public about his and his wife's childlessness. How else have you seen this happen? How could your own trials and disappointments bring you closer to others?
3. "There's an in-between time in every journey. In every pilgrimage. In every life." How can recognizing this fact help us face hard times?
4. This in-between time is always difficult, often lonely, and full of temptations to avoid the reality within it we must face. In such times, what avoidance strategies are you most tempted to use?
   - Excessive eating or snacking
   - Social media or other entertainment
   - Addictive substances like alcohol or other drugs
   - Pornography or other illicit content
   - Nostalgia
   - Sports
   - Other:
   (Snacking, social media, sports, and other activities

are, of course, fine in the right doses. We're talking about excessive use to avoid something.)

5. Is there something difficult in your life right now that God is calling you to face? What is it, and who will you approach to help you with it?

6. When do you think taking a "shortcut" in life is healthy? When is it not?

7. Reflect on the difference between medieval and Celtic concepts on pilgrimage (page 114). Are you looking for God's blessing in the destination or the journey?

8. Read Hebrews 11:13–16. How might viewing yourself as a nomad on pilgrimage to a "heavenly homeland" transform your view of life, pain, and the current season you're in?

CHAPTER 8: LOSING AND BIRTHING

1. Write down your first impressions from this chapter. Was there a story, phrase, or idea that could become a discovery for you?

2. How good are you at resting and relaxing?

3. Sheridan describes how comparing himself to others in the past has led to fatigue, even burnout. Do you ever struggle with comparison? If so:

   What aspects of the other person's life have you wanted?

   Are these things really yours to have?

4. What gifts and qualities in your life are you prone to forget by focusing on others' gifts and qualities?

———

5. "Busyness is a sure sign that we are living someone else's life and doing someone else's work." What work or aspiration are you doing or pursuing that isn't yours to do or pursue?
6. Read at least two of the following passages:
   - Matthew 5:3–12
   - Matthew 19:28–30
   - Romans 5:20–21
   - 2 Corinthians 4:8–12
   - 2 Corinthians 12:8–10

   What strikes you about the kind of people God blesses?
7. Sheridan gives some examples of people whose weakness, lack, or loss has birthed life-changing books, charities, and more. What other examples can you think of?
8. Dream a little. How could your weakness, lack, or loss bring healing, hope, and life to someone else? What lessons have you learned that you could share?

CHAPTER 9: GIFTS AND GRACES

1. Did you resonate with any particular character in this chapter? If so, why?
2. How aware are you of the gifts and talents you have? Here are the relevant biblical passages to show some of what's available. Which gifts do you think you have?
   - Leadership gifts: Ephesians 4:7–13
   - Motivational gifts: Romans 12:3–8, 1 Peter 4:11
   - Sign gifts: 1 Corinthians 12 and 14
   - Creative gifts: Exodus 31:1–11, 1 Samuel 16:13–23

Note: None of the gifts lists in the Bible is comprehensive. They are examples only, and there will be other abilities the Spirit gives. For more help on discovering your gifts, see www.sheridanvoysey.com /tmoutools.

3. Sheridan discovered something about his gifting by recalling what he *wasn't* good at or was bored by. What have you proven to be poor at doing? What activities soon bore you?

4. Sheridan suggests that in the world and in the church some gifts are recognized more than others. Would you agree or disagree with this? If you agree, which gifts do you see being ignored or undervalued?

5. Sheridan tells the story of Caedmon and his remarkable gifting to be a poet and songwriter. Notice how Hilda tested his gifts by giving him tasks to do. How have your gifts been tested and confirmed, or not, by others?

6. Hilda arranged biblical and theological training for Caedmon too. How are you developing both your gifts and general Christian knowledge?

7. Your gifts are given to you for a reason (1 Corinthians 12:7). Are you "stepping in the direction" of your gifts, using them to serve others and reveal God?

CHAPTER 10: PATHWAYS AND PROVIDENCE

1. What, if anything, stood out to you in this chapter? Reflect on why.

2. How different are you today to who you were . . .

As a child:

As a teenager:

Ten years ago:

3. In what ways would you like to be different ten years from now?
4. In your own words, what do you think it means to glorify God?
5. Could you be content having your contribution to the world left unknown or forgotten, yet known by God and pleasing to him?
6. "Affliction plus gifting can make magic happen." How have you seen this principle at work in others? How could you see it working in your life?
7. Sheridan suggests that it's in becoming more like Jesus that we become our true selves. Would you agree? (1 John 3:1–2 and 2 Corinthians 3:18 might be helpful reading.) How does this idea differ from secular approaches to personal development?
8. In what area of your life are you resisting God's efforts to make you Christlike?

CHAPTER 11: A NEW CREED

1. Note the parts of this chapter that touched or spoke to you.
2. Sheridan suggests we live to a rhythm based on the tides: flowing out in mission (work and action) and ebbing back in retreat (rest, prayer, and recreation). What practical ways could you apply this rhythm to your life . . .

Each day:

Each week:

Each month or season:

Each year:

3. Read Genesis 22:1–12, about Abraham's call to relinquish Isaac. Isaac was both a fulfilled dream (Abraham having a child) and an unfulfilled dream (God promising a whole nation: Genesis 15:1–5). Review the dreams you listed in question 3 of chapter 1. Could you, like Abraham, relinquish them into God's care?

4. What else might you need to relinquish right now?

5. Our culture tends to assess a person's life based on one or two big roles or achievements they attained. Sheridan comes to believe that our whole lives should be our *one big thing*. How might this change the way you think about the importance of both the "headlines" and the "fine print" of your life?

6. What is your response to "The Creed"? Would you write it any differently for your own life?

    (You can download a designed copy of "The Creed" at www.sheridanvoysey.com/thecreed.)

7. Review your answers to question 1 of each chapter in this reflection guide. Select from them three key lessons you will take from this book.

    Lesson 1:

    Lesson 2:

    Lesson 3:

8. How will you work these lessons into your life from today on?

JOURNALING PAGES

_____

_____

_____

_____

_____

_____

_____

_____

NOTES

CHAPTER 1: A SOUL ADRIFT

1. See Exodus 33:7–11, 1 Kings 19:11–13, Luke 2:36–38, and Luke 10:38–42.

CHAPTER 2: SAND AND STARS

1. Proverbs 8:22–32, author's paraphrase.
2. It has been said that all life rests on six numbers alone, a change to any one of them plunging the universe into chaos. See Martin J. Rees, *Just Six Numbers: The Deep Forces That Shape the Universe* (London: Phoenix, 2000), and Paul Davies, *The Goldilocks Enigma: Why Is the Universe Just Right for Life?* (Sydney: Allen Lane, 2006), chapter 7.
3. See Psalm 139:13–18.
4. The king was Oswy, and I have slightly paraphrased the story for clarity. The original is found in the Venerable Bede's eighth-century work, *The Ecclesiastical History of the English People*, Book III, chapter XIV.
5. See Matthew 10:29–31 and Psalm 139.
6. See Ephesians 3:14–19.

7. See 1 John 3:1.
8. Letter from Vincent van Gogh to Theo van Gogh, The Hague, May 14, 1882, accessed April 2018, http://www.webexhibits.org/vangogh/letter/11/193.htm.

CHAPTER 3: CAVES AND CROSSROADS

1. See Matthew 7:7–8.
2. Moments like these test whether we really believe verses like Proverbs 3:5–6 and Romans 8:28.

CHAPTER 4: VISIONS AND WHISPERS

1. John 3:8 (NIV).
2. When that first monk, Corman, found the English "stubborn," "barbarous," and uninterested in eternal things, the mission looked all but over. But to Aidan, Oswald's invitation was an opportunity that couldn't be ignored, especially given Corman's harsh temperament and poor approach. See Bede, *The Ecclesiastical History of the English People*, Book III, chapter V.
3. There are only three moments of clear divine guidance recorded for Cuthbert: a prophecy spoken over him by a child in his youth hinting at his future missionary role, his vision of angels on the night of Aidan's death, and a prophecy from Boisil, his mentor, about his one day becoming a bishop.
4. See Philippians 2:13 and 1 Kings 19:12.

CHAPTER 5: CASTLES AND ASHES

1. From the website of the earl's family home, Howick Hall: "The paintings behind the font and the altar were commissioned by Mabel, 5th Countess Grey, in the 1950's, and are not regarded as a success," www.howickhallgardens.org/churchhistory.php (accessed January 2017).
2. See Psalm 39:4–7, James 4:13–17.
3. Transcribed in Sheridan Voysey, *Open House Volume 1* (Sydney: Strand, 2008), 151.

4. This is what being made in God's image is all about, reigning over and tending creation under God. See Genesis 1:26–28 and 2:15.
5. 1 Peter 1:14–16 (NIV).
6. At the Synod of Whitby in AD 664, the Celtic church was ordered to observe Roman church ways in a number of areas, causing division among the monasteries, including Lindisfarne. A Celt at heart, Cuthbert nevertheless worked toward a unified church, patiently dealing with the complaints.
7. In AD 676 Cuthbert introduced laws on Lindisfarne and the Farne Islands protecting the eider duck and other seabirds from being eaten. In doing so, he became the world's first known conservationist.
8. Venerable Bede, *The Life and Miracles of St. Cuthbert*, chapter XXXIII.

CHAPTER 6: RIVERS AND STREAMS

1. John 15:1–2 (NLT).
2. Elfleda initially sought out Cuthbert for his prophetic powers, wanting to know God's plans for her royal family, but it seems a friendship formed. She kept the revelation about his future confidential for some time. See Bede, *The Life and Miracles of St. Cuthbert*, chapters XXIII, XXIV, and XXXIV.
3. Cuthbert and Herbert (also called Herebert) died on their separate island hermitages on March 20, 687—friends together in life and death. Bede, *The Ecclesiastical History of the English People*, Book IV, chapter XXIX.
4. Dorothy L. Sayers, "Why Work?" in *Letters to a Diminished Church: Passionate Arguments for the Relevance of Christian Doctrine* (Nashville: W Publishing, 2004).
5. Gilbert Meilaender, "Friendship and Vocation," in *Friendship: A Study in Theological Ethics* (Notre Dame: University of Notre Dame Press, 1981).
6. See William Perkins, *A Treatise of the Vocations*, 1605.

7. Aristotle, *Nicomachean Ethics*, Book VIII.
8. Proverbs 27:9.
9. John 15:15.
10. This story is found in Danusia Stok, ed., *Kieslowski on Kieslowski* (London: Faber and Faber, 1993), 176.
11. John 15:12, 17.
12. According to Jesus, every rule for living can be condensed into loving God and loving others the way we love ourselves (Matthew 22:37–40). "Love is the fulfillment of the law and should be everyone's rule of life," writes Carlo Corretto. "In the end it's the solution to every problem, the motive for all good." Carlo Corretto, *Letters from the Desert* (London: Darton, Longman and Todd, 1972), 25.

CHAPTER 7: THE SPACE IN BETWEEN

1. Ian Bradley brings this out in his book *Colonies of Heaven: Celtic Models for Today's Church* (London: Darton, Longman & Todd, 2000), chapter 6.
2. Hebrews 11:13–16 was an important passage for Celtic Christians. We are nomads and foreigners in this world heading for a heavenly homeland. In this sense a physical pilgrimage was a small echo of the entire life journey of a Christian.
3. Gerald O'Collins, *Second Journey: Spiritual Awareness and the Mid-Life Crisis* (Leominster: Gracewing, 1995).

CHAPTER 8: LOSING AND BIRTHING

1. All stories from Bede's *The Life and Miracles of St. Cuthbert*. Washed feet: chapter XVIII. Lifted burdens: XII. Quelled fire: XIV. Turned water into wine: XXXV.
2. Bede, *The Life and Miracles of St. Cuthbert*, chapter IX.
3. All stories from Bede's *The Life and Miracles of St. Cuthbert*. Cured by touching Cuthbert's clothes: chapter XXIII. Cured by wearing his shoes: XLV. Cured by water used to wash his body: XLI.

4. Bede, *The Life and Miracles of St. Cuthbert*, chapter VIII.

5. David Whyte, *Crossing the Unknown Sea: Work as a Pilgrimage of Identity* (New York: Riverhead Books, 2001), 118.

6. See Proverbs 31:10–31, particularly verse 16 (buying property, planting a vineyard), verse 18 (making a profit), and verse 24 (marketing garments).

7. Proverbs 31:23. In biblical times, elders sat by Jerusalem's gates giving guidance on spiritual and civic matters.

8. See Matthew 5:3–12, 19:28–30, and 5:5.

9. See Romans 5:20–21.

10. See Matthew 18:3, Daniel 1, Mark 12:41–44, Matthew 5:13–16.

11. See 2 Corinthians 12:8–10.

12. The redemption of Paul's trials is summed up in this profound phrase: "So then, death is at work in us, but life is at work in you" (2 Corinthians 4:12 NIV). For a general summary of Paul's sufferings see 2 Corinthians chapters 4, 6, and 11.

13. They're called the Recycled Orchestra of Cateura: www.recycledorchestracateura.com. A film was made about them in 2015: www.landfillharmonicmovie.com (both accessed July 14, 2018).

14. Joni and Friends: www.joniandfriends.org (accessed July 14, 2018).

CHAPTER 9: GIFTS AND GRACES

1. Bede's World has since been renamed Jarrow Hall.

2. In Eastern and Orthodox churches. After the Gregorian calendar was introduced in 1582, Roman Catholic and Protestant churches started following a different method of computing the date of Easter.

3. Bede, *Ecclesiastical History of the English People*, trans. Leo Sherley-Price (London: Penguin Classics, 1955), 329.

4. Benedict started this project first in Monkwearmouth, about seven miles south of Jarrow, building St. Peter's Church in AD 674. Upon its success he expanded to a second campus, creating

St. Paul's in Jarrow in 682. The two establishments were seen
as one monastery—the Monkwearmouth-Jarrow Monastery—
although Jarrow became the better known due to Bede's fame.

5. See Thomas Cahill, *How the Irish Saved Civilization* (New York:
Anchor Books, 1995).

6. Lists of spiritual gifts can be found in Romans 12:4–8,
1 Corinthians 12:12–31, and Ephesians 4:7–13 and summarized
in 1 Peter 4:10–11. But these are not complete lists of all gifts
the Spirit gives. The gift of creativity, for instance, is seen in
Bezalel and Aholiab's craftsmanship: Exodus 31:1–11.

7. Bede, *The Life and Miracles of St. Cuthbert*, chapter XI.

8. Bede, *The Life and Miracles of St. Cuthbert*, chapters XXIV and
XXVII, and XXIV and XXVIII, respectively.

9. Bede, *The Life and Miracles of St. Cuthbert*, chapters XXXII,
and XII and XV, respectively. For other examples of Cuthbert's
healing ministry see chapters XXV, XXX, XXXI, and XXXII.

10. Hilda was a fascinating figure. Trained by Aidan, she built a
mixed monastery of monks and nuns to great success. Bede
writes of her outstanding piety, her training no less than five
bishops—more than any other monastery—and her governance
of the monumental Synod of Whitby in AD 664 (see his account
of her in *Ecclesiastical History of the English People*, Book IV,
chapter 25). Hilda wasn't the only female church leader of the
time. Ebb was a friend of Cuthbert who led a mixed monastery
just north of Lindisfarne. And when Hilda died in AD 680, we
find Cuthbert's friend Elfleda taking over as abbess of Whitby.

11. While Caedmon wrote prolifically the rest of his life, only the
song from that dream survives—Caedmon's Hymn, the oldest
song in Old English we have. Bede recounts Caedmon's story in
Ecclesiastical History of the English People, Book IV, chapter 24.

12. See Exodus 31:1–11.

13. See 1 Samuel 16:13–23. As for David's songs, they remain today
as many of our Psalms.

14. See 1 Corinthians 12:21–25. Paul took the Christians in Corinth

to task for celebrating those with miraculous abilities—like the ability to heal—while downplaying less spectacular talents.

15. 1 Corinthians 12:7.

16. 1 Corinthians 12:7 (THE MESSAGE).

17. It's interesting to note that both supernatural and ordinary gifts are listed side by side in the relevant passages (see 1 Corinthians 12:27–31 in particular).

18. We are told to seek spiritual gifts (1 Corinthians 12:31, 14:1 and 12), but the Spirit ultimately decides which we get based on where God wants us to serve (1 Corinthians 12:11 and 18).

CHAPTER 10: PATHWAYS AND PROVIDENCE

1. With the body's remarkable ability to regenerate itself, it has been said that we experience head-to-toe rejuvenation every seven to ten years. This process is seen most commonly in hair and nails, which naturally grow when cut, but happens in other parts of the body too. Our red blood cells are replaced every four months, while some white blood cells last only hours or even milliseconds. Taste buds are replaced every ten days, liver cells every three hundred to five hundred days, surface skin every two weeks, eyebrows every sixty-four days, and our skeletons are replaced once every ten years. For a handy overview of this, see "The Continuum of You" on *New Scientist*, www.newscientist.com/round-up/body (accessed July 14, 2018).

2. C. S. Lewis fans owe a lot to Walter Hooper, Lewis's last personal secretary, who upon Lewis's death in 1963 dedicated himself to keeping the great writer's work alive. To date Hooper has written or edited more than thirty books on Lewis's life, writings, and personal letters, delving into archives to bring out new and fascinating material. It has been noted that J. B. Phillips, an equally gifted writer of the day, lacked someone like Hooper to keep his work public. Most of Phillips's fine books have now fallen out of print.

3. See Exodus 33:18–20 and 34:6–8, Psalm 96:6, Isaiah 6:1–5, Matthew 17:18, Hebrews 1:3, Revelation 1:12–18, and Psalm 8:5.
4. John 17:6.
5. John 17:7.
6. John 17:4.
7. See John 12:23–28 and 17:1.
8. Bede, *The Life and Miracles of St. Cuthbert*, chapter XLII.
9. Bede, *The Life and Miracles of St. Cuthbert*, chapter VII.
10. Godric's story is told in the twelfth-century book *The Life of Saint Godric* by Reginald of Durham.
11. These and other fanciful stories were recorded in Symeon of Durham's *Libellus de Exordio atque Procursu istius, hoc est Dunelmensis, Ecclesie* (compiled 1104–7), and Reginald of Durham's *Libellus de admirandis beati Cuthberti virtutibus* (compiled in the 1160s and '70s).
12. Cuthbert's attitude to women is a tragic example of this rewriting of his story. By the twelfth century women were no longer permitted near Cuthbert's shrine at Durham Cathedral, a line even drawn on the floor that they were not allowed to cross. Symeon of Durham tells of women struck dead or going mad for disobeying this rule, as well as the "backstory" to it—Cuthbert supposedly ordering the rule after disciplining some unruly nuns at Coldingham, bringing an end to mixed monasteries. This is in stark contrast to the picture painted by Bede of Cuthbert's close relations with women—visiting his foster mother Kenswith, meeting with abbesses and queens, his friendship with Elfleda, and the many stories of his healing women.
13. See James 1:2–4, Romans 5:3–5.
14. See Amos Yong, *Theology and Down Syndrome: Reimagining Disability in Late Modernity* (Waco: Baylor University Press, 2007). Yong writes as an academic theologian with personal experience, his brother Mark having the condition.
15. See 1 John 3:1–2.

16. See 2 Corinthians 3:18.

CHAPTER 11: A NEW CREED

1. The embroidered stole, maniple, and girdle are recorded as gifts of King Athelstan when he visited Cuthbert's shrine at Chester-le-Street in AD 934—the only surviving pieces of Anglo-Saxon embroidery in England. The other relics mentioned are dated to the seventh century and believed to be owned by Cuthbert himself.

2. Produced by the monks at Wearmouth-Jarrow in the late seventh or early eighth century, the St. Cuthbert Gospel is now Europe's oldest surviving bound book.

3. You can see high-resolution images of key Lindisfarne Gospels pages, including those mentioned, at www.bl.uk/turning-the-pages/. I am indebted to Michelle Brown for providing a vocabulary to describe the unique art of the Lindisfarne Gospels also. Her 480-page book examines them in detail: Michelle P. Brown, *The Lindisfarne Gospels: Society, Spirituality and the Scribe* (London: British Library, 2003).

ABOUT THE AUTHOR

Sheridan Voysey is a writer, speaker, and broadcaster on faith and spirituality. His other books include *Resurrection Year: Turning Broken Dreams into New Beginnings* (shortlisted for the 2014 ECPA Christian Book of the Year), *Resilient: Your Invitation to a Jesus-Shaped Life*, and *Unseen Footprints: Encountering the Divine Along the Journey of Life* (2006 Australian Christian Book of the Year).

Sheridan has been featured in numerous TV and radio programs, including *BBC Breakfast*, *BBC News*, *Channel 5 News*, *Day of Discovery*, and *100 Huntley Street*. He is a regular contributor to faith programs on BBC Radio 2 and other networks, and speaks at conferences and events around the world.

Beyond this, Sheridan is a husband to Merryn, a walking buddy to his dog Rupert, a lover of soul and funk, photography, and dark chocolate, and a pilgrim in search of wisdom and wonder. He resides in Oxford, United Kingdom.

To subscribe to Sheridan's podcast *More Than This*, visit www.sheridanvoysey.com.
And join him on social media:
Facebook: www.facebook.com/sheridanvoysey
Twitter: @sheridanvoysey
Instagram: www.instagram.com/sheridanvoysey

CONTINUE THE JOURNEY

There are many lessons hidden within *The Making of Us* story, lessons that can help you become the person you are made to be. To help unearth and apply them to your life, we have created a series of practical exercises, podcasts, and other application tools. Find them at **www.sheridanvoysey.com/tmoutools**.

Perhaps a greater tragedy than a broken dream is a life forever defined by it.

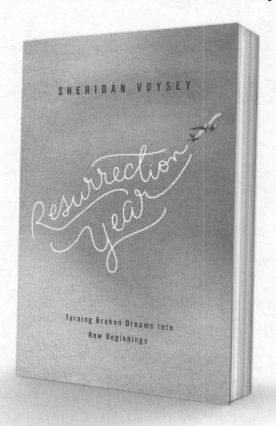

SHERIDAN VOYSEY

Resurrection Year

Turning Broken Dreams Into
New Beginnings

"Sheridan Voysey writes from experience—there is life after the death of a dream. Your dream may be different, but the road to resurrection will be similar. I highly recommend it."

—Gary Chapman, author of *The Five Love Languages*

"*Resurrection Year* is a gift that will breathe life and hope into many who have faced a broken dream."

—Darlene Zschech